Body Wisdom®

A Guide to Rediscovering
Your Relationship with Food,
Trusting Your Intuition
and Becoming Your Own Health Expert

By Cara Carin Cifelli
Foreword by Tristan Thibodeau, MS

LIMITED LIABILITY
AND DISCLAIMER OF WARRANTY:

Editing: Tristan Thibodeau, MS

DEDICATION

When the idea of writing this book first came to mind, I was writing it for the twenty-year old version of myself. At the time, I was really lost and confused about how to eat and take care of my body. The information in this book is what I wish I knew back then but took me my entire life to learn.

In reality, I wrote this book for anyone struggling to be at peace with food. For anyone confused about how to feed themselves in a way that makes them feel nourished and excited to be alive.

This book is for those struggling to love and trust their bodies whether they think it "looks good" or not.

CONTENTS

ACKNOWLEDGMENTS

First, I want to acknowledge my dear friend Tristan, who wrote the forward to this book and was by my side throughout the entire writing process. Without her loving support, dedication and time I am pretty certain this book would have never been published. We met through Instagram which seems to be *the* way to meet like-minded people in your industry these days and I am so very grateful for her. Over the course of a year she has slowly become one of my most trusted friends.

And to everyone who has supported and believed in me along the way.

To my mom and dad, despite their concern for my ability to earn a living as a health coach, have supported and cheered me on the entire time. They have always done whatever they could, with the resources available, to help me find my footing in life.

To my closest friends, many of whom believed in me, even when I didn't have faith in myself. Nirinjan, Dara, Christina, Kyle, Ashton, Yvette, Digger, Erin, Juan, Ben and Zach. You all have always had my back and I am truly grateful for our friendship.

And to my boyfriend, Brent. Thank you for many things but mostly for making me laugh.

Thank you to all my peers and those in my online and social media community. You bring so much joy and purpose to my life.

And lastly, to every single women who has ever been made to feel like she was not enough because of her body. You are enough.

FOREWORD

Ladies, (and fellas if you're reading this) let's be honest, 2016 onward has been a major doozy.

Fighting the persistent patriarchy, courageously standing up to declare #metoo, and demanding equality for all women on the race and gender spectrum has allowed us to step into our feminine power to a depth unfelt by generations of women before us. Yet there is a relentless force that continues to degrade and belittle us. It convinces us that we are unworthy of love, respect, or dignity unless we subscribe to its stringent rules. The tragic part is that we unknowingly participate in this systemic sickness that serves to keep women small and restricted. This force is known by many names, but is notoriously known as disordered eating.

As women, we are hard-pressed to engage in a conversation or ingest information from the media that does not involve belittling our bodies to an unrealistic expectation of an invisible waist size, a thigh gap, perfect tits, or a Kardashian booty (still not convinced). Imagine what you could accomplish and experience in this life if eating "the right" food and your body image no longer consumed your time and energy. In Body Wisdom, Cara teaches women how to escape the torturous wheel of disordered eating, body image issues, and restriction so that you can tap into the innate intelligence that your body possesses to help you experience life to the fullest. Cara and I both share a past of painful eating disorders, body image issues, and the restrict-binge cycle. The parallels between our stories are spooky at times, but I have found that most women share many common experiences because the way in which our society belittles our bodies are very consistent amongst the many social media platforms.

This book is a guide to finally releasing our society's control over your mind, body, and spirit. It's time to stop believing the lies that you are not worthy or "enough" if you do not look a certain way. It's time to release all that no longer serves you so that you can step into your fullest power and accomplish what you were put on this earth to do. Body Wisdom is your guide to coming home to who you are and leaving behind toxic and limiting beliefs. If you put in the work that this book lays out for you, only good things will come into your life. All you have to do is believe that you are worthy of everything your heart desires and know that your effort will pay off.

It's time to be free babes!

All my love,

Tristan

1
WHAT IS BODY WISDOM

"At the end of the day, your body is the best consultant in the room."

—Dr. Mark Hyman

Food plays a leading role in all of our lives. Not only in a spiritual, cultural and communal way, but also in developing who we are as individuals. Everything we ingest gets digested, metabolized and assimilated into our bodies and then affects who we are and how we show up in the world. What we eat either lifts us up, gives us energy, vitality and fuels our creativity, or it pulls us down, making us bloated, dull, fatigued, irritable and even sick

In essence, how we produce, prepare and consume food has one of the greatest impacts on our wellbeing. Yet, navigating the world of food and nutrition these days is *not* easy. Given the endless amount of resources available, you would think that reliable answers would be easy to find. Yet with so much *mis*information out there it's hard to know where to begin, or who to trust about what the heck to eat. On top of it all, we have unachievable expectations of beauty that lead to disordered relationships with food and poor body image—both of which just add to the drama and confusion.

All of this BS makes this whole eating thing *so* complicated. Body Wisdom is the key to saying goodbye to all the food drama and instead, learning to tap into your unique bio-individuality around the foods that make you feel your best. Before we are able to dive into cultivating your ability to decipher for yourself what is healthy, we first need to address the barriers that many of us struggle with when we attempt to transform our relationship with food. So let's first talk about the forces that you are up against that tend to distract and confuse your built-in Body Wisdom.

Barrier #1—Confusing Science

Abiding by scientific research regarding what is best for our body often seems like a fool-proof way to eat and live well. We can try to apply what cutting edge scientific research tells us, but literally every food-related health claim can be debated by a quick Google search. One study may show that soy causes breast cancer,[1] while another may prove that it's a healthy protein choice.[2] When everybody is tofu-fighting it is hard to enjoy your miso soup in peace.

With a barrage of conflicting scientific data and varying opinions from health experts like doctors, coming at us each day regarding how, when and what to eat, we are left second guessing our own innate ability to choose the best food for our bodies. The reality is that we are all so individually unique that blanket statements, even when they are "proven valid" by research, can be more confusing than they are valuable. Simply put, you might be very different than the "average person" in any given study used to make various health claims.

Barrier #2—Marketing Tactics

When we enter into the chaotic and misleading environment of the grocery store, our ability to apply what we believe to be true regarding nutrition and well-being becomes nearly impossible as we are pushed to purchase products that appear to be "healthy". At the end of the day, grocery stores are a business and the food industry takes advantage of this profitable opportunity by adding confusing and often misleading health claims, even sometimes using shame-based language on labels to increase sales.

Food packaging can say things like "gluten free" or "guilt free" in an effort to appear like a superior option without making you question the nutritional information on the back. The number of unrecognizable ingredients in packaged and processed food is greater than most people's Instagram followings, which makes the ability of understanding what you are actually eating similar to reading an entirely different language. With all of this confusion, it's no wonder we tend to brush right past the nutrition label and take what the front of the box says at face value. But, eating well *can* be made simple. While there are so many layers of unnecessary complexity to nourishing your body, throughout this book I will help you become fully armed to decipher what is actually healthy for you versus what is just good marketing.

Barrier #3 — Sensationalized Diets

Not only can it be a real struggle to know *what* to eat, it's also difficult to *enjoy* what you eat when we are being constantly bombarded by confusing inconsistencies about what is "healthy." Every week there seems to be a new fad diet that promises to be the key to food freedom and body liberation. So is Paleo the answer or is it Vegan? Or the newly coined "Pegan." Is it Bulletproof or Whole Foods Plant-Based? It is Ketogenic or low fat? Or high carb, Slow Carb, low carb? Is it Fruitarian, Vegetarian, Raw-Food Vegan, Clean Eating or Ayurvedic? What is funny is that none of these are wrong but none of them are necessarily right either — it's truly individual. Throughout the following chapters, I will help you see through the veil of information that sensationalized fad diets use to keep you latched on and investing in their credo. You will develop the tools necessary to figure out what way of eating is right for you.

Barrier #4—Societal Pressures

Occasionally we may find that our food choices are dictated by external influences such as fear from judgement from others or societal pressures to look a certain way. When we attempt to abide by these impossible standards, we create excess stress and in the process often lose the connection between what we eat and how we feel. We can be so wrapped up in the nutrition recommendations from the external world that we have no capacity to hear the information being sent to us from our body's intuition. This makes living a healthy lifestyle a chore for so many of us because we are so damn confused about how to nourish ourselves, and far too often are even made to feel insecure about our food choices. This is *not* a healthy way to eat or live.

Couple this struggle with the unbearable pressure put on us to have perfect bodies and it's no surprise that so many of us have very unbalanced relationships with food and distrust with our bodies. The issue with establishing intuition around food while resisting societal pressures to look a certain way is made even more confusing as we attempt to navigate the vast array of "food" products made available to us.

This confusion layers on additional stress to our already stressed out society. The endless piling on of stress compounds over time to affect our mood, eating habits, productivity, overall wellbeing and fulfilment in life. What's even more soul crushing is that this added stress has been scientifically proven to affect our health and even our weight. When studies compare present day life to that of 20 years ago, it has been observed that modern Americans have higher levels of stress and therefore have a more difficult time losing excess weight.[3] But our fixation with weight-loss is where a lot of the problem lies.

Barrier #5 – Diet Cultures Ideal of "Perfect"

Our obsession in America with having the "perfect body" and losing weight has misdirected the focus from "how to live a healthy lifestyle" to "how to lose weight." All the fat-phobia and body-shaming happening in our society has resulted in us constantly pursuing weight-loss *in the name of health*. But our weight is not really the best indicator of health despite what we are taught.[4] Consequently, we care less about how we feel in our bodies and care more about what our body looks like.

This insecurity with our appearance can have us fall victim to fad diets and "get thin quick" schemes, ultimately zapping the joy right out of life. Sometimes, we'll resort to extreme measures and take advice that could end up hurting our health and longevity in the long run. Not to invalidate anyone, but it seems like everybody has a theory on how to best lose weight or the right way to eat. There are varying opinions from bloggers, doctors, authors, family members and celebrities so it's hard to know who is actually "right" about what we all should be eating.

On top of that, there is no one right way to eat forever. As women, we go through serious hormonal changes throughout our life which make our cravings for certain foods shift and our need for various nutrients fluctuate. Even day to day our hunger levels change, so saying that there is a right amount to eat each day (AHMM, 2000 calories or 3 large meals or 6 small meals or within a 12 hour window) is bullshit and only takes us further away from listening to our body. Not only that, but our environment, stress level, and palate can change so it is very unlikely that you will eat one way for the rest of your life. And to be completely honest with you, I disagree with people that preach that there is only one way to eat and live. The right way to eat is the way that makes you feel good in your body.

That's it. The truth is that there is no one right way to eat for everyone.

Now that you are aware of all that you are up against in creating a way of eating that helps you feel your best, know that I truly do understand how confusing it can be to try to live a healthier lifestyle that honors your body's needs and wants. At the end of the day, the way of eating that is best for you is completely unique *to you*. Before discovering the bliss that is Body Wisdom, I was constantly influenced by what I read and heard from the outside world. For years I struggled with an obsession with food that made every day a challenge until I discovered that so many of the answers I was looking for were already within the beautiful and powerful machine that is my body. I just had to be willing to listen to it.

Which brings me to why I wrote this book:

- ▶ to help other women who are struggling with disordered eating and dieting, and-
- ▶ to provide you with a road map for developing your own Body Wisdom that is grounded in intuitive eating, mindset medicine and holistic nutrition.

I believe that there is the perfect amount of nutritional education in this book that will allow you to confidently tune out all the rest and trust that the remaining answers lie within your mind, body and heart.

My Hope for You, Reading This Book...

My hope for you is that this book strengthens your ability to interpret the signals from your body and use intuition when making food choices so that you are able to decipher what is a healthy way to eat for *your* body.

My hope for you is that you begin to listen to and trust your gut so that you don't have to constantly second guess what is best for you. This will transform your outlook on health, and I'm so stoked for you to learn how to establish this relationship with your body.

My hope for you is that you give yourself permission to stop dieting (or pursuing *wellness, weight-loss* or *clean eating*) forever so that you can enjoy what you eat and know what it feels like to be nourished.

My hope is that you learn to trust and respect your body. At the same time, I hope you learn to accept and love it because regardless of the changes you want to make by developing Body Wisdom, loving and accepting your body is necessary for the real work to begin.

My hope is that you are able to develop your own unique Body Wisdom so that you can live vibrantly and *"do you."*

My hope for you is that you honor your body daily. That you truly listen to what it tells you. This is fundamental to you in your pursuit of creating behavioral and lifestyle shifts that help you become the brightest version of yourself.

Where Your Journey Begins

This begins by developing the understanding that your body is a complete system as opposed to the belief that it is just a bunch of individual parts. In doing so, you will begin to develop the awareness of how different foods make you feel. Ultimately, this awareness is power as it will allow you to decide how you want to feel *every single day*. Focusing on how you feel will allow you to take the focus off of how you look. As I am sure you know, when we are self-conscious of our body, it's hard not to obsess about food. So when the focus is shifted from how we look to how we feel, the act of eating takes on an entirely new meaning. Let this book help you feel empowered through your food choices so that you can trust your intuition and live a life where you feel your best.

If I have learned anything through my journey to my own Body Wisdom, it is that it is a very personal journey. Food is unique to each of us, and this book is designed to be a tool to help you develop your own understanding of your bio-individuality so that you wake up excited to take on the day and create the life you want.

Having a body that is full of vitality allows us to redirect our energy from struggling with our health and body image to authoring our most authentic life. Unfortunately, most people don't know how good their bodies are meant to feel because they are trapped in a disordered eating cycle. After discovering how incredible my body felt when I ate and exercised intuitively, I realized that the purpose of my previous struggle with food was so that I could share the knowledge I gained through my journey with others.

We are not supposed to constantly feel fatigued, have headaches, not be able to think straight, be bloated or sentenced to a life with chronic illness. We are not meant to obsess and analyze every bite of food we eat either. And lastly, we are not meant to hate or distrust our bodies. Our bodies are incredibly powerful machines and sacred containers we get to experience life through. When fed well and cared for properly we have the ability to feel amazing throughout our lives.

A Little Back Story

I know first-hand how trying to overcome food obsession, yo-yo dieting, and all the emotional issues that follows suit is like being thrown down into the gauntlet. There were days where I thought I would never get out of the food prison I found myself in, hell, that I *PUT* myself in. I internalized this struggle with food for so long that it began to reflect how I perceived my self-worth, which ultimately lead me to believe that killing myself might be the easier way out. I know that might sound dramatic but I felt like my food prison had no windows to the outside. It was truly suffocating.

I was in this cage where I would always get seduced by the latest and greatest diet. Every time a new one would come out I would willingly pledge allegiance to it. I always thought this one would be the final push I needed to make me love my body and help me lose any excess unneeded weight for good. Looking back, I can see clearly why my relationship with food was such a mess, especially given the world we live in, but now I am someone who just eats in a way that feels best to my body. It's that simple. Healthy living does not need to be stressful or loaded with guilt and shame.

Getting here took some trial and error and it also did not happen overnight. The journey began over a decade ago and started by cultivating some serious self-love and body acceptance. After crying on the bathroom floor following a massive, but very typical binge and purge episode, I realized that I could no longer live like *this*. And by *this*, I mean yo-yo dieting, my eating disorder, hating my body, and feeling like crap with a slew of uncomfortable health issues. I had finally had enough. In that moment of sorrow and self-pity, I decided that I was worth fighting for. I entered into recovery and healing and made a conscious choice to honor my body and finally get this whole food thing figured out.

A pivotal point in this process happened when I adopted a fully Whole Foods Plant Based lifestyle or veganism, which was polar opposite to how I had been eating. It truly was therapeutic for me at the time, which I explain in depth later in this book. Eventually I added eggs back in, then selectively other animal products, but my point is that I've tried to follow other people's guidelines about how to eat. What I discovered is that the right way for me to eat was unique to me and can change from day to day. And ultimately our body knows better than anyone on what and how we should be eating.

After going on my first diet at age 15 and then developing an eating disorder that followed me into my mid-twenties, it's safe to say that my life has always been heavily influenced by food to some extent. Now my obsession with food has evolved from a form of self-deprecation into a powerful form of self-expression and love. It's the vehicle I use to connect with and be of service to the world. So in writing this book about food, nutrition and Body Wisdom, I hope this is the last "diet book" you ever feel inclined to read. Honestly though it's not even a diet book, but I'm pretty sure you get me.

Acquiring Your Tool Kit

The journey to the promised land of feeling incredible requires a diverse tool kit that will equip you to mend your current relationship with food and your body. The primary tool that I work with is *holistic nutrition.* Holistic means to look at things as a whole, so this book will present all sides of the food/diet/nutrition paradigm and along the way, equip you with a variety of tools that you will be able to become an expert at utilizing.

The first tool is developing the understanding of how the body is a complete system, and the types of foods that are available to us to strengthen this system. This can be complicated by the marketing hoops our society makes us jump through, so I will help you develop the ability to understand when a claim is true, when it is just marketing, or when it is founded in outdated science.

The second tool will help you determine what foods work best for your body. We will explore foods that can cause stress, digestive *dis-ease* and other undesirable symptoms. This knowledge will help create awareness on what foods could be keeping you from feeling full of life. It is not meant to tell you what to eat and not eat, rather give you some clues to help you start to pay attention to what foods are making you feel vibrant and nourished, and what foods are making you feel fatigued and sluggish. In essence, this section will connect you more to your built in Body Wisdom.

The third tool will help us understand where our cravings come from. In doing so, we will explore the psychology of our cravings and the biology of what drives us to eat so that you can understand why you might find yourself eating healthy all week long only to binge the weekend away, i.e. why dieting and calorie restriction does not work and how to escape the binge-cleanse cycle and break free from the *diet mentality* and say bye-bye to *diet culture*. Ugh, I really hate diet culture and I cannot wait for you to say *bye Felicia* to it all. (and if you do not get that reference please Google® it, its hilarious).

The fourth tool is intuitive eating. I will teach you the steps to intuitive eating and how it shifts our relationship with food to something that is easy. During the learning process, you will have to be mindful in order to apply these new skills, but with enough practice you will become effortlessly healthy. You will soon learn what it feels like to live an intuitive lifestyle, and it is the most liberating experience in the world. To help get you there I will teach you the necessary mindset shifts and how I reframed the way I looked at food which allowed me to change the way I viewed and lived my life.

The fifth tool is cultivating and understanding of the ethical dilemmas we currently face within the health and food industry. I will dive into the ethics (or lack thereof) of our food industry and how my anger with our current situation ignited my eating disorder recovery. It made eating about something that had nothing to do with me and my body size which was so unbelievably freeing. It may or may not resonate with you, but it contributed to me shifting my trust from the outside world to my own body.

Your final tool will be forged by putting to practice all that you have learned. I'll share my favorite Body Wisdom Pillars, and wrap everything up with the easiest recipes for snacks and meals that you can throw together during the week for quick, delicious eating. This is going to be so much fun!

The Ethos of Body Wisdom

This book is not about restriction, sacrifice or following a fad diet. It is designed to help you find balance and wellbeing by mapping out an easy approach to living a healthy lifestyle that is right for you.

This book is about teaching you how to trust and respect your body. And maybe by the end of it you might love your body too.

This book is designed to help set you up for discovering what works for you so that you can create a lifestyle that allows you to feel strong, healthy, powerful and beautiful. Our relationship with food has the ability to be simple and free flowing, we really can eat with ease and grace. It doesn't have to be forced, confusing or complicated.

This book is designed to provide just enough information so that you to feel confident to leave your controlling mind and enter into the wisdom of your body. It will give you the freedom to get in touch with your gut instincts and intuition so you can stop overthinking every bite of food you eat.

This book is about helping you change your life for real, and forever.

The Problem is the Damn Wagon

When we are unable to stick to a diet or workout regime, our society makes us believe we have failed in some way, thus leading us into a shame spiral that puts us right back into old habits. What we often don't realize is that it's more likely that these diets and regimes failed us, rather than us failing them. Without this understanding, we find ourselves on a pendulum swing going from one extreme to the other. What most people don't realize is that when we "fall off the wagon" that doesn't mean we are weak or unmotivated. Rather it is the belief that there is a wagon to fall off of in the first place that holds us back.

What if we just removed the damn wagon?

My theory is that when we tune out the world's opinions about how to live and eat and tune into our Body Wisdom, we discover how to eat and move in a way that is easy to maintain and dare I say, *enjoyable*. Following a diet that promises weight loss or purchasing a workout program guaranteed to give you six-pack abs might help you in the short-term, but what happens for the rest of your life? Creating weight-loss and even health in a false setting, meaning one that does not resemble how you plan or want to live out your life, often yields temporary results and disappointment.

It is so common for people to frequently jump from weight loss fad to weight loss fad because they are desperate to find a quick solution to a long-term problem. Or perhaps you go through periods of eating well and not eating well. If it has taken months or years to get to the state of health you are in (if that's even the case, you might actually be healthy but think you are not good enough because of *diet culture*) then a 30-day slim down or drastic calorie restriction is not the answer. These fads are often short-term solutions that do not set us up for long-term results. It is a vicious cycle that leaves us completely off balance with low self-esteem that is wrapped up in shame and guilt about our bodies.

Wanna know a little secret? Your body has the perfect plan for health already inside it! Yet ignoring our Body's Wisdom means we put more faith in commercialized health than the intuitive ability that is built-in.

The takeaway here for you: You have got to *do you*.

Returning to Our Intuitive Energy

As Dr. Anita Johnston explains in her book *Eating in the Light of the Moon*, we have abandoned our feminine energy which is rooted in our intuition and emotions. Instead, we have transitioned into a more masculine energy which utilizes a logical and rational approach to eating. Instead of trusting our body's ability to guide us to foods that are in line with our unique selves, we rely on elaborate diet plans that tell us when, what, and how much to eat. Instead of paying attention to when our body craves physical movement, we rely on intense exercise regimes that have been created by the fitness industry to give you the "perfect body", but our bodies are already perfect.

These recommendations trap us in a cycle where we calorie restrict, track points or macro count, over or under eat, and ignore signs from our physical body. We attempt to control and manipulate our bodies with our mind, when we should be tapping into our intuition that is grounded in our individuality and feminine energy.[5]

Every time we eat, we experience a variety of sensations, emotions, and feedback that are meant to help us observe how different foods make us feel. If we learn to trust our bodies and fill up our plates with food that makes us feel vibrant and nourished (both physically and emotionally), the act of intuitive eating becomes incredibly simple.

Health and wellness is already programmed into our body machine, but it is our job to tap into this programming by listening to the internal signals and clues they send us.

This is Body Wisdom.

Chapter 1 ACTION STEPS

Discovery 1. Think about YOUR unique version of health and what Body Wisdom means to you. What does it encompass and entail?

Discovery 2. Where do you feel most confused and lost in the world of health, nutrition and knowing what, when and how much to eat? Do you feel blocked by any or all of what I had mentioned? What clarity are you hoping to get from reading this book?

2
HOW WE HOLD OURSELVES BACK

The magic happens just outside of your comfort zone."

—unknown

T uning into our Body Wisdom might *sound* easy. It is possible that you fully understand what I mean by it intellectually but the *how* may seem more elusive. Last chapter we talked about the various things in our society and world that often block us from developing Body Wisdom. Before we explore how to implement actions and habits that strengthen and cultivate your Body Wisdom, we need to explore how we internally stop ourselves as well.

We first have to start with the actions we are currently taking and the thoughts we are currently having that are holding us back from tuning into our Body Wisdom. I know that you are probably skeptical, nervous, anxious, or chomping at the bit to get started on transforming your relationship with food and your body. You may be thinking to yourself:

▸ *Gosh, how do I let go of trying to control my body after all of these years of judging everything I eat?*

▸ *How do I take the guilt, shame and stress out of eating and living healthfully?*

▸ *How do I stop constantly looking for the perfect way to eat that leads to health, longevity and ideal body composition?*

▶ *How do I let go of the fear of weight gain or of not following a regimented plan of eating or counting points?*

▶ *How do I heal my relationship with food?*

▶ *How do I discover how to truly eat the foods that make me feel most nourished, vibrant and alive without feeling restricted and deprived?*

Learning to have a balanced relationship with food means being willing to move through the fear of the unknown. So many of us are afraid that if we stop controlling our food that we are going to go bat shit crazy and *eat all of the things*. We think that the opposite of control is no control and in a way it is, but not in the way you might think. Imagine not feeling controlled by food, imagine feeling the freedom to eat what you want, when you want and not have it mean anything about who you are as an individual.

Imagine having a natural inclination towards foods that make you feel good. Imagine loving your body so much that you want to take care of it right now regardless of the changes you want to make. Imagine having a plate of nachos or a cookie and putting a metaphorical period at the end of the experience because you feel satisfied and full.

Imagine being so in tune to your body that when it's craving kale salad you eat a kale salad, and when it is craving pizza you eat some pizza- with no stress, no moral superiority or demoralization, no need to adjust what you eat tomorrow- just flowing in and out of what to eat to make you feel nourished, satisfied, loved, and alive in each moment.

Imagine being fully in tune with your beautiful body machine and all of its wisdom. To help get you there we have to explore what barriers we put in our own way to tuning into Body Wisdom. Here are some of the most common barriers to get you started on your process of unearthing your own self-constructed blocks.

Block #1: Food Rules and Nutritional Dogma

Are you willing to let go of all the rules you have about how, when and what to eat? And since we're on the subject, do you know what the rules are that you have anyways? Do you have conscious awareness of them and how they are running your life and relationship to food?

Some examples of rules are: eating between a certain window of time, like no food after 7pm, or do you believe that there are "good foods and bad foods" or foods that are "ok to eat and not ok to eat," or sugar is the devil and addictive, or carbs are fattening. These are the types of rules we create as a result of what the outside world tells us and it truly messes with our ability to choose food because we want to eat it and it will satisfy us. It also makes food choices a morality issue which leads to guilt and shame.

Part of developing Body Wisdom is having the courage and the trust to step outside of your comfort zone and be uncomfortable with not knowing what is going to happen by letting go of all the rules you tend to follow. You have to be willing to stop following them and instead listen to what your body tells you. That means if it wants a piece of bread, you eat a piece of bread and enjoy every single bite of it. While there is benefit to having nutritional insight, it is possible that we let it override what our body tells us. So are you ready to ditch your food rules?

Chances are, most of these rules came from outside of yourself. The nutritional information overload of the outside world clogs up our internal and intuitive information system. When we are so consumed by what others have told us to do, it's hard to listen to our body. Over the years as we have tried various things with little to no lasting success, we start to distrust ourselves and our body. This blocks Body Wisdom. So, wipe your slate clean, ditch the rules and beliefs that you have, and start fresh with your body.

Block #2: Fear of Weight Gain

Almost always part of what holds us back from developing Body Wisdom is a fear of weight gain. You may also have some health issues and body *dis-ease* you want help healing, but in your pursuit of health are you also hoping to lose weight and manipulate the way your body looks?

If so, how afraid are you of gaining weight?

No really, think about this. Consider for a minute that so much of your problems with food and way of eating are wrapped up in the fact that you are petrified at the idea of gaining weight or not losing more weight. Look, I am not saying that developing Body Wisdom automatically means you will gain weight, I have absolutely no clue if you will or won't, but I do know that it is a possibility. Unfortunately, in order to develop Body Wisdom you have to be ok with the potential of weight gain and welcome the opportunity for your body to work its own magic. Who knows, you could very well lose weight but either way, you have to become weight neutral during this process.

If you have to try really hard to stay at the weight where you are right now, chances are that you might not be at your natural Set-Point, or the weight range at which your body runs optimally and is most comfortable. If you truly want to become an intuitive eater and develop your Body Wisdom, you have to be willing to trust your body to do what it needs to do. Trust your body not only to regulate the millions of mechanisms going on inside of you at any given moment, but you especially need to trust it to regulate your weight. Even if you have health issues that you want to heal from, I am willing to bet there are some fears about your body size tangled up in them.

Honestly, what is going to happen if you *do* gain a little weight? What does it mean about who you are and your life? If the worst case scenario is that *you gain a little weight*, is it worth having the mental space and freedom that Body Wisdom provides? Is it worth feeling ease and grace around food? Is it worth trusting and respecting your body? And if you are someone that has been engaging in behavioral and lifestyle choices that have resulted in weight gain, it's possible that developing Body Wisdom by adopting new habits and ways of being will result in weight loss. That said, we have to not be afraid of what will happen with our weight if we want true freedom from food and Body Wisdom.

As someone who has moved passed that fear, I am here to tell you that it absolutely is worth it, but *you* have to make the decision for yourself. I cannot choose it for you and if no longer pursuing the perfect body is not ok with you, then that is ok too. It is one hundred percent your right to choose.

However, obsessing about and wanting to control our weight is a huge part of why eating healthfully and normally is so challenging for you. If you view eating a salad as "being good" and a meal that will help you manipulate your body it's no surprise to me that you do not love vegetables and enjoy eating them in abundance. And if eating pizza is "bad" and going to "make you fat" I am not surprised that you feel guilt and shame from eating it and often binge on it.

So I have to ask, what is on the other side of weight loss? What is it that you want that you think you cannot have because you "have weight to lose?"

To help you answer this question fill in this sentence:
"When I am thin I will _____."

Some common responses from my clients are:
When I am thin I will be confident.
When I am thin I will finally find a partner that loves me.
When I am thin I will wear a swimsuit.

When I am thin I will finally be happy.
When I am thin I will be enough.

I hate to burst your bubble but you do not need to lose weight to attain any of those things. Don't get me wrong, our society absolutely treats people different based on size, but why are you fighting the fat when you could be fighting against the oppression and prejudice of weight stigma? Plus, there are plenty of people of all shapes and sizes who are living fully expressed lives, filled with peace, joy, happiness and confidence who do not fit society's arbitrary and unrealistic beauty ideal.

I can imagine that some of you might be having a really hard time reading this right now. You might actually be questioning if you should even continue reading this book because what you were hoping to get out of developing Body Wisdom was weight loss. While I am not *anti-weight-loss*, I am very much *anti-weight-focused*. Obsessing about our weight makes it nearly impossible to develop Body Wisdom because it perpetuates a disordered relationship with food. It makes food about changing your body size and not about nourishing your body and thriving in all areas of your life.

Are you willing to let go of your fear of weight gain and your goal of weight loss in order to develop Body Wisdom?

Barrier #3: Lack of Body Acceptance

If you are reading this, then I am willing to bet that you are not happy with your body. Maybe it is your size and shape that bothers you or perhaps you have a health issue like IBS (Irritable Bowel Syndrome) or PCOS (Polycystic Ovarian Syndrome) that you want to heal. Maybe you have both. Either way, accepting your body as it is right now is necessary for you to develop Body Wisdom.

When I first approach the idea of body acceptance with clients, they immediately interpret it as giving up or meaning that they are content with how things are. That is not the case but as long as we continue to see it as something that needs fixing it's challenging, if not impossible, to develop Body Wisdom. When we choose to not view our body as "good or bad" or "right or wrong", and instead accept our body just the way it is right now, we allow ourselves to work in alignment with it, rather than against it. It allows us to be a neutral receiver of the information it sends us instead of being a judgmental peanut gallery.

Choosing to accept your body, and if possible *respect it*, right now does not mean you do not want to make changes. It does not necessarily mean you will stay fat or get more fat, or that you will become more unhealthy, it just means that you accept it as it is right now. Period. The earth is round, the sun is the center of our solar system, the sky is blue and this is your body. It's just a matter of fact. Having this attitude allows us to not act in reaction to it. Coming from a neutral place of acceptances allows to create how we want to live each day.

Despite your objections, it is absolutely possible for you to accept yourself as you are, right now which will help get you closer to loving yourselves down the line, too. Believe it or not, other people are capable of loving you the way you are now, but how you feel about yourself absolutely affects how you interact with others, which affects how they interact with you. I know that when I am not confident, I am not outgoing, friendly or kind to others. I don't mean to be, but I absolutely come across as standoffish and not friendly. Whereas when I am confident, I am a more enjoyable person to be around and naturally make more friends. So how we feel about ourselves does impact how others treat us. So if we think that *all the things* are wrong with us then others are going to pick up on that and often mirror our energy.

Typically, our objections to body acceptance takes away our ability to feel empowered. Rather unconditionally loving your body, meaning not making your love conditional based on size, shape or health status, will open you up to a sense of freedom and put you in a better position to develop Body Wisdom. If loving your body seems impossible work towards acceptance first, which does not require you to like anything about your body just truly get that this is the body that you have right now.

Time for a Little Tough Love

Staying stuck in the mentality that you have to be a certain size for your life to work or to be the way you want it to be is an insecurity that is keeping you from living a fully expressed life. Chances are, it is the thief of so much potential joy in your life as well as a convenient excuse that allows you to play small. What I mean is, we often use our weight as an excuse for why we aren't living the life we want instead of taking responsibility and ownership over creating the life of our dreams.

So are you willing to let go of control to see what happens? Are you willing to face some discomfort, just experiment and play with me for a bit while you read through this book? Are you willing to turn down the volume on the outside world and tune into your body? Are you willing to release your expectations and desires for weight loss and try accepting your body right now?

Are you willing to see your symptoms and body sensations as your Body Wisdom speaking to you? Anything that comes up for you from your body be it bloating, headaches, irritability, digestive issues and the like are your body's way of telling you something. Are you willing to listen to it, interpret it and then act in alignment with it?

This book is not meant to tell you exactly what to eat and how to live so you lose weight. In fact all of the nutritional information in this book is to be interpreted as weight neutral. I do share facts, statistics and research because I do think it has value but it is meant to help you develop the same tools necessary for Body Wisdom that made a difference for me in my own journey. Just try it on, keep an open mind and remember you can take it or leave it.

There are millions of resources out in the world telling you exactly what to do.

"Just follow this exact diet plan and you can live happily ever after."

That's not what this book is, and if that's what you expected, #sorrynotsorry. This book is to help you figure out what will work for you by listening to your body.

Just a heads up, shit might get a *little* messy.

This process is not going to be perfect or easy. It's going to require that you do some work and think differently about food, health and weight loss. I do believe that there are nuggets of information and wisdom in these pages that will empower you to do that.

Are you ready to develop Body Wisdom?

Chapter 2: ACTION STEPS

Discovery #1: What are your rules around food? What are the health and nutritional dogma that you constantly think about? For example: "I can't eat sugar, it's bad for me" or "carbs are bad" or "I can only eat XYZ macros, calories or points each day" or "I have to work out 3-4 times a week or I am lazy" etc.

Discovery #2: Is your fear of the unknown holding you back? Is your fear of weight gain keeping you white-knuckling your way through each day? If so, what is truly going to happen and what does it mean if you gain weight or don't lose more weight? Why is it such a horrible thing?

And most important are you willing to be ok with whatever happens if it means peace, joy, freedom, acceptance, trust with your body and food freedom?

Discovery #3: What are your objections to body acceptance? Can you genuinely accept your body knowing that doing so does not mean you can't also want to make changes? Doing so actually puts us in a more empowered position to make the changes we want to make because we are working with not against our body.

3
OUR BODIES ARE A SYSTEM

"The part can never be well unless the whole is well."

—Plato

Now that we have a good understanding of what barriers are standing in your way to tuning into your Body Wisdom, give yourself some time to reflect upon the internal and external "realities" that are interrupting your ability to develop your unique relationship with your body. Once you are able to clearly observe and analyze the barriers from others and that you have created for yourself, you will be able to see all the ways that those barriers have been popping up in your daily life and robbing you of the joy you deserve. It's time that we cleaned the slate so that you can start to create your new reality.

Before we get started on the heavy lifting, I want to give you a head's up on what you can expect in the following chapters. The first part of this book is designed to help free you from the external oppressions that pollute your connection to your body. The latter parts of this book will help you with the internal dialogue we run each day and the stories we have about our bodies and health that are hindering our connection to our Body Wisdom. So let's get started with understanding what our beautiful body machine is, how it operates, and how we can pay attention to its natural rhythm.

Our Bodies Are a System

Our bodies are these wicked cool machines that are busy at work all day every day helping us to live the life of our dreams. It's very easy to take for granted the magic that is our body and all the things that it can do because we were born into them, we didn't have to earn them. We have a brain that tells our heart to beat, and lungs that inherently know how to breathe. We have eyes to see, ears to hear, teeth to chew, a liver to cleanse, kidneys to purify, legs to move, arms to hug, fingers to touch, and a stomach to digest all of the delicious things we eat.

It isn't until we become sick that we get confronted by the physical limitations presented when our body is not feeling or operating at its best. When the machinery that is our body stops working optimally, it throws us off center. If we are light headed, irritable, have aches and pains, a headache, foggy brain, sore throat or are fatigued, it's hard to be our most spirited, dynamic, and energetic selves. We are robustly connected to our physical bodies and we function best when all parts work in tandem. [6] We are made up of an insanely complicated system that consists of several different tissue types, bones, organs, water structures and integral elements that are all interconnected. Aristotle, the Greek philosopher, said that "the whole is greater than the sum of its parts" and that could not be more true than when we are referring to the mental and physical aspects of our bodies.

To exemplify how we often overlook the complexity of our body machines, let's start with one of the most vital systems in our body: the digestive system. Your digestive system consists of over 7 organs including the mouth, esophagus, liver, stomach, pancreas, small intestine and large intestine (which includes the rectum and anus). All these parts make up your gastrointestinal (GI) tract and work together to help you digest and assimilate food into nutrients and compounds your body can use to keep you healthy and glowing from the inside out. What you eat is ingested, digested and absorbed into the body by way of our gut and microbiome. This then affects everything from how we feel physically to how we operate mentally. You simply need to listen to the news, read a magazine, or pay attention to our national health reports to know that we are currently experiencing a nationwide malfunction in the health of our body machines. We are breaking down left and right, and the answer to this degradation may simply require us to tune into our intuition and listen to our gut.

Tuning into the Gut-Brain Connection

As Dr. Mark Hyman explains in his documentary "Broken Brain", our gut which has been coined the second brain, may play an even bigger role in mood regulation and overall health than what we previously recognized. He explained that we now know that there is a bi-directional highway of communication between our brain and our gut called the "Vagus-nerve." Dr. Raphael Kellman, who was featured in the film, explained that science has recently discovered that the gut sends up to 400 time more messages to the brain than what the brain sends to the gut.[7] This means that what we eat is literally participating in the communication with our brain and directly influencing how our brain works. These new findings indicate that the food we eat and the health of our digestive system directly affects our mood, motivation and outlook on life in addition to our overall health and wellbeing.

What the health and medical community is starting to realize is that our current approach to treating *dis-ease* by treating the symptoms as opposed to focusing on the root causes has lead us to a health epidemic. This epidemic is perhaps the most apparent when observing the increased prevalence of mental health disorders in our country. According to the ADAA (Anxiety & Depression Association of America), 18.1% of the American population is dealing with anxiety with most cases being treated with prescription medications and neglecting the role of diet in mood status entirely.[8] The body is a whole, and yet the idea that a mood disorder is related to the food you eat and the bacteria in your gut is a new idea that is yet to be unanimously accepted amongst our medical community.

Luckily, cutting edge scientific research is changing the way we understand the relationship between diet and whole body health and a new model of healthcare is in the process of being created.

Where the West and East Collide

Western Medicine has become known as *Modern Medicine*, because as a system and social structure, it has been the most recent addition to the realm of Medicine and Health Care. Eastern Medicine which utilizes a *Holistic Approach* is rooted in ancient tradition and wisdom that developed over centuries of observation and practice. A new area of medicine known as *Functional Medicine* combines the best practices of both Western (modern) and Eastern (holistic) Medicine. Functional Medicine utilizes a systems approach to disease and illness while still taking advantage of the best life-saving procedures that have been developed by Western Medicine. One form of medicine is not necessarily better than the other, as Western, Eastern, and now Functional Medicine are important and have played a role in our survival and expansion as a species. They do however excel in very different arenas.

Western Medicine, sometimes described as "evidence-based medicine," has used the scientific method and research to create its treatment plans.[9] It takes a *symptom-based* approach to treating various injuries, illnesses and diseases with surgery, pharmaceuticals and radiation. It is not a type of medicine that focuses on prevention, rather its focus is on treatment because it profits more on this model, but we'll talk about our insurance system more later.

Although I sometimes have resistance to Western Medicine because my beliefs agree more with a Holistic Approach, there are times when our country's medical system has truly kicked ass. Our body is a machine that on occasion has broken pieces and malfunctioning parts than need to be tended to. Western Medicine has greatly excelled at making some previously life-threatening repairs such as fixing broken bones, providing organ transplants, removing brain tumors or conducting open heart surgery widely available. It is responsible for discovering penicillin, and administering vaccines that have helped eradicate or prevent the spread of deadly diseases like Smallpox or Polio. While I am not trying to get into a debate on the ethics of vaccines and antibiotics, you can't deny the role they have played up to this point in wiping out some diseases that once threatened our life and longevity on planet earth.

Part of my apprehension with how we address health care in this country is that it does not always take a well-rounded approach to preventing or healing *dis-ease* and optimizing health.

If we…:

▶ have a heart problem we see a Cardiologist,
▶ experience a foot and lower leg problem, we see a Podiatrist,
▶ have a lung issue we are sent to a Pulmonologist,
▶ are having problems with cognition and memory, you see a Neurologist.

Western medicine treats the body part by part, as opposed to honoring how each piece influences the health of the whole system. With that being said, having access to specialized practitioners who focus on the complexity of each smaller system can be incredibly valuable in understanding the intricacies of how our whole body system works. However, I believe that we need to treat illness and disease from a holistic approach because everything is connected inside our body by means of cause and effect. As we have observed in countless occasions both in scientific research and the subjective experience of the individual, treating our bodies part by part often results in a slew of unwanted side effects. Shifting a handful of aspects within one piece of the system results in shifts within other aspects of the system, because our bodies operate in a synergistic manner. So although one pill resolves the symptoms of one problem, it can create a slew of symptoms due to a lack of synergy amongst the entire body machine.

This loss of synergy often results in even more medications being prescribed to treat the side effects of the first medication, and this cycle tends to continue until you find individuals on 5, 10, even 15 medications. I am not saying that pharmaceuticals have not been or cannot be very beneficial for certain conditions, however I want to acknowledge that they are sometimes over prescribed, used to treat symptoms rather than the root cause, and should not be used as first line care for the majority of health concern, especially for those that can be remedied through diet and lifestyle modification.

How Broken Body Wisdom Leads to Broken Health

If you need a concrete example of how medications can be a slippery slope, let's return back to the example of mental health and diet. Let's say that you are battling depression, which is known by many to be a very difficult and painful mood disorder (if any of you reading this are suffering please know you are loved and there is hope). What is commonly prescribed is a pharmaceutical drug to help correct chemical imbalances in the brain known as antidepressants. Like most medications, the changes they create can result in other side effects in the body. Antidepressants have been known to cause jitters, dry mouth, weight gain, decrease in sexual desire, fatigue, insomnia and anxiety[10]. These side effects may result in additional prescriptions to remedy the discomfort caused by the antidepressants, but will not solve the underlying root cause of depression in the first place.

Although antidepressants have been very helpful for some people and taking medication can be a form of self-care when they are truly necessary, this approach does not always consider how other parts of the body may be influencing the state of your mood and brain health. It also doesn't truly honor your Body Wisdom, but instead masks what the body is trying to tell us (obviously there are exceptions to this in extreme cases of mental health so be sure to follow your doctors order if you are taking prescribed medication).

Your body's intuitive wisdom is a phenomenal feedback mechanism to tune into when determining the root cause for health conditions such as depression and anxiety. This could not be more true than with the example of how the gut communicates with the brain and determines our mood state. The health or diversity of the microbiome in your gut can create symptoms of a depressive state. In fact, 90% of serotonin, which is one of our most important neurotransmitters for mood status, is produced in our gut and this chemical messenger affects our mood, appetite, social behavior, and sexual desire.[11] There are over 100 million neurons inside the walls of our digestive tract and as we mentioned earlier, it communicates with your brain through a bi-directional highway. [12] And trust me, your gut has **a lot** to say. Despite these groundbreaking discoveries, there is still a massive mismatch in what research indicates about the relationship between our gut and mental health and what is applied in current medical practice.

The Mismatch of Modern Science and Medical Application

I believe one of the most frustrating aspects of modern medicine is felt in the amount of time that it takes our medical system to put into application novel principles from the latest and greatest scientific research. Our understanding of the gut as our second brain and the role that it plays in our mental state and immunity is still very much at the forefront of scientific research, but very little of this information is currently being applied in patient care. Although new scientific data is widely available to the public, practicing doctors are often unaware of the new research that shows how antidepressants and our diet affect the diversity of bacteria in our guts, thus affecting our good mood neurotransmitter production. [13] Most doctors rely on the original information that they were taught in medical school which instructs them to use antidepressants to treat a patient for mental illness. This typically leaves doctors unaware of the role of nutrition because we are only just beginning to learn about the powerful role different foods have on our gut bacteria and how they influence our mood. We will dive much deeper into the role of our gut in a later chapter so get excited because it is so, so cool!

How the Band Aid Approach Neglects Body Wisdom

Although having a medication that can quickly improve our state of mind can be helpful, (and sometimes life-saving) it can also lead to a dependence and negative side effects. By ignoring our Body Wisdom and neglecting the root cause of mental illness, the degree to which our dietary and lifestyle choices factor into developing these issues is often overlooked. One reason why we are seeing advancements in nutritional science so quickly, especially regarding food and gut health, is because we are starting to realize that our reliance on pharmaceuticals does not actually heal the body, but rather creates a need for additional medication and sometimes creates new problems.

Take hormonal birth control as another example. There are many reasons why a woman might want to take birth control besides its intended purpose of preventing pregnancy. These reasons might include improving irregular periods, cramps, acne, unwanted hair growth and PCOS (Polycystic Ovary Syndrome). While the pill can help improve or alleviate these *symptoms*, it doesn't address the root cause, and often leaves many women unaware of other solutions such as using diet and lifestyle to balance hormones naturally. To take or not take birth control pills is a choice that each women has the right to make, yet most women are completely unaware of the side effects that ignoring the root cause of hormonal issues can create.

Dr. Jolene Brighten, a Functional Naturopathic Doctor specializing in women's health, explains on her website that "the big problem with using birth control to treat symptoms is that it is only covering up an underlying issue and potentially allowing the symptoms to get worse or the underlying disease to progress." This is another example of how well-intended doctors may have over prescribed a medication to women because the science was lacking on how there can be unintended consequences to taking hormonal birth control. It's true that women in the 1960's and beyond were stoked to have a way to not get pregnant. However, what women and our medical system did not realize is that in many ways birth control completely overrides the body's ability to self-regulate its hormone production, which destroys a sense of synchronicity within the body as a whole and also creates unwanted and perhaps harmful downstream consequences that the woman must then address.

According to Dr. Brighten birth control can contribute to leaky gut, nutrient deficiencies and can affect the body's ability to naturally detoxify itself. So although in theory having a medication to help us feel sexually liberated and prevent unwanted pregnancy is a good thing (in my opinion), prescribing birth control for conditions beyond what it was originally intended for masks other important signals from the body and can cause other unintended issues as a result.

Hormonal birth control is so regularly prescribed that we are led to assume that there is no other way to naturally mitigate conditions such as irregular periods, hormonal issues, cramps, acne and PCOS. Yet, if we turn to Body Wisdom and a holistic approach, there are other ways to improve or reverse symptoms without prescription drugs. Through viewing the body as a system, we can see that everything can impact a women's cycle including diet, lifestyle, physical activity, stress level and self-care practices. While this may seem daunting and overwhelming, I encourage you to view this approach through the mindset of a hands-on experiment where we are able to pay attention to the signals our bodies sends us in order to find solutions to what ails us naturally.

The body is constantly sending us feedback in the form of either good health or problematic symptoms. As our world continues to become more chaotic, stressful, and "busy", we are continually losing the ability to focus on what *good* feels like. We have replaced our Body Wisdom with a cold and broken medical system that is structured to further disconnect us from our ability to care for ourselves and heal according to our original value to "do no harm." Choosing to instead tune in to communication with your body may be overwhelming at first, especially if you have lived the majority of your life without listening to what your body is asking for. Opening that line of communication may also open the floodgates of neglected information that your body needs you to hear. Yet the more time that you are able to invest in restoring this line of communication, the less overwhelm you will experience when listening to and applying your Body Wisdom.

A modern example of how to apply your Body Wisdom to alleviate hormonal irregularities is to consider experimenting with a method of creating balance within your monthly cycle, known as Cycle Syncing. Cycle Syncing is a holistic approach to syncing your lifestyle with your menstrual cycle, and it has really helped some women dealing with symptoms related to their periods and hormone irregularities.

By digging deeper into how our body works at a biological level and observing the impact our daily choices and environment have on our hormonal balance, we are able to approach hormonal abnormalities from a *systems approach* as opposed to covering up symptoms with hormonal drugs.

Alissa Vitti, the author of *Woman Code*, is a pioneer in this regard as she talks about the flow of life, how we as women go from peaks to valleys and hormonal highs to lows throughout our cycle. Much like the seasons, women go through four different phases (Luteal, Menstrual, Follicular and Ovulation) throughout the month, and our hormones are at different levels in each phase. By making changes in our lifestyle, decreasing stress, eating balanced high fat and low glycemic foods and exercising in a way that supports our hormones, we can balance our body and potentially decrease all the flare ups naturally without using a prescription pill that has side effects.[14] Spreading the word that women can take control of their bodies through diet and lifestyle changes (aka tuning into Body Wisdom) is slowly making waves just like the connection between gut health and brain health. As this knowledge becomes more widely accessible to women, my hope is that we not only decrease our desire for quick fixes, but that our need for prescription medications decreases. These changes would allow our medical system to once again focus on true patient care and well-being as opposed to masking symptoms and turning a profit on prescriptions.

How Our Broken Medical System is Creating Broken Health

Both Dr. Brighten and Dr. Hyman are at the forefront of the transition in our healthcare system to use both modern medicine and holistic nutrition together. They have been quick to adapt to scientific research and observation, but the application of this research is slow to permeate throughout the remainder of our medical system as a result of a few key structural issues.

Structural Issue #1—Lack of Nutrition and Lifestyle Education in Medical School

There are many barriers that practicing doctors face in staying up to date on scientific research that supports using diet and lifestyle modification as primary care. The first barrier is experienced while pre-med students are still in medical school. Most medical students receive on average only 23.9 hours of nutritional education while in medical school. [15] Not only is this amount of time insufficient, but the actual content regarding nutrition education is in most cases completely outdated. Kelly Leveque, a prominent Health Coach and Nutritionist in Los Angeles said in an interview on the Mind Body Green Podcast that one of her post-graduate classes at UCLA was still teaching outdated nutritional science information such as margarine being a healthier alternative to butter and other sources of saturated fat like coconut oil or animal products.

As someone who eats saturated fat daily, I know the positive impact it has on how I feel. In 2015 the FDA regulated the use of trans fats that are commonly found in processed foods, such as margarine. Trans fats are formed through a process called *hydrogenation* and anytime you see the words "partially or fully hydrogenated oils" in the ingredients on a product label, it is a clear indication that the product contains trans fats. Science has proved that trans-fat increase LDL (bad) cholesterol and lowers HDL (good) cholesterol therefore increasing your risk for heart disease.[16] And in general will probably not make you feel that great after eating it. I dive a little deeper into the education in this country and how it is skewed by industry influence in the last part of this book.

Additionally, the education and curriculum in medical schools can significantly lag behind current scientific research because new discoveries are made every day and it is very challenging to keep costly materials like textbooks and curriculums up to date with that rate of change. Several programs in medical school would need to be entirely redesigned and upgraded which is incredibly costly and very time consuming. I am by no means saying that this is an excuse for medical education to lag behind important scientific discoveries, but this is very much the reality of why there are so many incongruities between research and medical application in patient care.

Structural Issue #2 — Limitations with our Insurance Model

While I agree that scientific advancement should technically translate into better patient care, most doctors are too overwhelmed with the stress of balancing patient visits and insurance paperwork to have any hope of staying up to date on cutting edge scientific discoveries. The insanely high patient load, fast-paced consultations, endless amounts of insurance documentation, pressure from the pharmaceutical industry to prescribe their medication, and varying size of a medical staff that requires management all act to prevent physicians from devoting their time to self-education and a different approach to patient care. We have become so frustrated with the current state of our medical system that we blame individual physicians for their lack of education, as opposed to focusing on the medical system itself as a whole which overworks and overloads doctors with tasks that distract from patient care. It is by no means the fault of any individual medical professional. When we shift our perspective, it becomes easier to understand why the most recent discoveries in health-related research take so long to be applied within our medical system. It would require practicing doctors to take it upon themselves to stay up to date on the most recent research between work, family, loved ones, and personal passions. Given their average patient load, the staff they manage and the amount of insurance papers they need to fill out, it is understandable why they might not be able to do so. Based on this reality, there needs to be a shift in how our medical system helps patients apply life-saving lifestyle change and how we can each take matters into our own hands by tuning into our bodies.

A New Professional That is Providing Hope in Re-establishing a Holistic Approach to Health Care

This is why the emerging profession of Health Coaching is becoming an increasingly valuable extension of our health care system in this country. According to the American Medical Association "Health coaching is a collaborative approach to care that informs, engages and activates patients to take a prominent role in managing their health. By bridging the gap between the physician and patient, health coaches can help practices improve patient engagement in their care, leading to healthier patients with better outcomes."[17] When a patient is supported by a health coach they are able to slowly implement changes in their life within the supportive relationship of the coaching agreement. Ultimately, this leads to an increased benefit in their overall health and wellbeing by empowering the individual to create a healthier lifestyle. Additionally, working with a health coach can decrease the amount of medical care and individual needs which saves the patients, doctors and insurance agencies money, time and lives.

A health coach is a trusted ally in the journey and process of prevention and treatment. A health coach who works in conjunction with an individual's primary care physician can help to implement behavioral and lifestyle adjustments with the patient over time that yield steady and meaningful results.

Together, the doctor and coach can decrease the need for medication for issues that can be resolved with lifestyle and nutrition modification.

Ultimately, what a coach can do is help you discover your own unique Body Wisdom by guiding you through changes and helping you to adapt to new discoveries you make about your body as you begin to adjust the food you eat and how you live.

Healing your body requires that you prioritize your own health and well-being before anything else. Often health coaches are not covered by insurance so money is a barrier for many people. That said, working with a health coach is a very real investment, but the return on your investment is that you gain the ability to work *with* your body instead of *against* which is absolutely life-changing. When you begin to prioritize your own well-being, the desire to invest the time, effort, and financial resources becomes less of a struggle and more of a desire. Basically, it's an investment that will pay massive dividends over time.

Healing your body naturally can be incredibly liberating when you work with a professional whose job is to make the entire process of change more intuitive and less of a struggle for you. Yes, it can take real work and acceptance of change to transform your health without pharmaceuticals, but it is also a very rewarding process. Working with a Coach and healing your body naturally is not a magic pill or a quick fix, but is a way that we will be able to become the source of our own body's transformation and create a long-term solution.

Alternative methods to healing are typically not fast acting, which could be why so many of us willingly and eagerly use medication without first looking for other options. We generally take a medication with the upfront understanding of how much you need to take to produce the desired result. We are comforted by the "guarantees" that medications provide, but this instant gratification often comes at a lofty price. However, if we approach change with less judgement and impatience, the benefits gained from slowly changing the way we eat, think and live each day will without a doubt improve our health in the long term....you just have to be willing to work for and wait for the results.

Re-establishing Body Wisdom by Utilizing a Holistic Approach

We have learned to find comfort in the instant results of pharmaceuticals so that we can spend less time on developing our own health and more time on our obligations. I am not against medication when medically necessary, but I am a big advocate for the healing nature of food when we work in alignment with our Body Wisdom. When we have a headache I completely understand taking an ibuprofen to alleviate the pain. Yet if we approach the headache from a holistic perspective, we can reframe the pain as an indication of cause and effect. This then enables us to shift our perspective from alleviating pain because it is discomforting into being curious about why the headache is there in the first place.

This is how we tap into our Body Wisdom which then informs our knowledge and awareness of how to prevent future headaches from occurring. We want to treat symptoms and ailments quickly and easily. Life is hard enough, and I'll be the first to admit that it does take time and effort to heal the body naturally and find the underlying cause of our ailments. Yet investing this time back into yourself is the best preventative medicine in which you can actively participate.

Since the body is such a complex systematic machine, discovering how to heal ourselves through food is very much a trial and error process that unfolds slowly. It takes time, observation and a willingness to try new things. We have to pay attention. When we use food and nutrition as our primary tool instead of pharmaceuticals, we can become our own health experts who are empowered by our choices each day. Although eating a single salad won't immediately make us healthy, each meal represents an opportunity to eat in a way that creates a higher vibration inside of us. If we do this consistently for long enough we can heal our guts and then learn to listen to them.

Taking Personal Responsibility for Your *Dis-Ease*

I not only had to discover what foods worked for me, but I had to learn to trust myself around food. And that took a while. I spent 3 years healing physically, mentally and emotionally which might seem like a long time if you are wanting to heal right now. But we cannot let the time it will take to accomplish a goal stop us because that time will pass regardless of whether or not we take action.

It truly is each of our own responsibilities and potentially within each of our own power to create absolute magical shifts in our bodies. As we have begun to explore (and will dive deeper into throughout this book) the food we eat and how we eat is the foundation upon which the rest of our life can grow. Arming ourselves with tools and knowledge is part of the process, but when we feel victim to our bodies it's understandable why we sometimes feel at a loss, are not sure of the value of healing food and look to a medication to help solve the problem.

While this is not an all-out-attack against pharmaceuticals, it is my own personally held belief that we can heal ourselves naturally with time, consistency and effort. Especially since it can be difficult to determine what is at the root of our suffering. Yet being honest with yourself and getting vulnerable to pieces of life that we don't want to face is the best way to get to the root of what is causing *dis-ease*. I know this through my own experience.

How I Learned to Get to the Root of My *Dis-Ease*

In addition to the anxiety and depression medication and birth control I was on when I was in my late teens, I regularly suffered migraines, constipation, bloating, arthritis and insomnia. I never considered that what I was eating or how I was eating was the source of these problems. Even though I was only a teenager, I regularly needed over-the counter pain medication and excessive caffeine just to get through the day and sometimes I even resorted to laxatives or taking a fiber supplement to ease my digestive woes.

At the time I did not have the awareness of what foods were triggering my anxiety, pain, fatigue, and digestive unease. It was beyond my understanding that diet sodas, iced tea with sweeteners, ice cream, and cheese were making me feel bad. Aside from the ice cream, I thought these foods were "healthy" choices for my body. It wasn't until I started experimenting with eliminating certain foods from my diet that I was able to experience a change in how I felt. Essentially, I started to tune into what my body told me after I ate certain things, i.e.—my Body Wisdom.

For years I drank diet soda because the outside world told me it was *the better choice for weight-loss and for health.* I ate cheese and dairy products because it was *low carb, high in protein and good for my bones.* I never considered the fact that my body might not thrive on these things. I hadn't yet heard of Bio-Individuality and had never considered just listening to my own body's signals. I was very wrapped up with what the outside world was telling me.

When we are constantly told that certain things are good for health from what appear to be authoritative sources, we often don't question their validity. It's why we can go on consuming foods for years that don't make us feel good and we struggle to bridge the gap on our own. While struggling with my eating disorder I was also not feeling good in my body. While I very much had a massive fear of gaining weight I simultaneously wanted to get to the source of all my health issues and body discomfort.

I had this epiphany that the ailments I was dealing with could be the result of what I was eating. For me it was a new thought that food was more than just a function of gaining and losing weight rather affecting who I was and how I was showing up each day. My acne, bloating, constipation, low energy, foggy brain, migraines, insomnia and general discomfort in life might be because of what I put into my body. Like, how could the foods I eat *not affect* how I feel? I know, *bold idea* so I decided to start listening to my body more.

Gluten-free was starting to become popular in the media so that was what I chose to eliminate first. As a result, consequently I naturally increased my animal and dairy consumption. While it was not my intention to increase consumption of animal products, anytime you remove a food group you tend to automatically increase others. After about 2 weeks my symptoms were noticeably worse. My acne looked like chicken pox, I was so bloated that my jeans didn't fit, it was really hard to poop and my joint pain was so intense that I couldn't walk without it hurting.

It was clear that gluten wasn't the culprit of my body pain so I decided to nix the dairy. Within 3 days I was an entirely new human.

Ok, not *entirely* but I started to notice a difference. New pimples weren't popping up, my jeans fit comfortably again and walking was easier. Within a month my skin had cleared up significantly that people were asking what my secret was. My stomach was flatter, my digestion was better, and the inflammation in my joints decreased so much that I literally cried. Up to that point I couldn't remember the last time my wrists, ankles and knees didn't hurt upon waking up or going to bed.

As perplexing as it is for a teenager to have arthritis, it became alarmingly clear that dairy was the source of so much inflammation and pain in my body. In retrospect, I realize now that these first steps in paying attention to how my body reacted to different foods was massively influential in healing my eating disorder and later structuring my future career as a holistic Health Coach. This experience is what set me on the path to where I am now. Helping others cultivate a connection to their internal Body Wisdom so they can be the healthy M.F. they want to be.

After some time I decided that I wanted to give up all sodas and artificially sweetened things including package protein bars and sugar-free candy. Within a couple of weeks my migraines went away completely. It's not that I don't occasionally get headaches from stress or tension, but the bedridden, sensitive to everything, pounding in my head experiences are a thing of the past. This profound improvement in my overall well-being led to me to dig a little deeper into scientific research and nutritional information that was outside of the world of weight-loss.

Common Foods that Create *Dis-Ease* and Disconnect Us from Body Wisdom

As it turns out, there are common symptoms associated with the consumption of some foods or "food-like" ingredients that are often overlooked by the *diet culture* in America. As I experienced with my reaction to these foods, symptoms that manifest from sensitivities or intolerances often result in either self-medication with over-the-counter drugs, or prescription medications to manage symptoms.

Below is a chart of some commonly consumed foods and their known side effects so that you can start to observe how your body responds to these compounds. I am not saying to never eat these things or to put them on some *"off limits list"* rather sharing this information so you can start to tune into your Body Wisdom and see if you experience these discomforts as well.

Food or Food-Life Stuff	Known Symptoms From Consumption
Artificial Sweeteners	Depression, drowsiness, joint pain, headaches, weight gain, irritability[7]
High Fructose Corn Syrup	Weight gain, decrease satiation signals to brain, leaky gut, diabetes
Artificial Coloring	Hyperactivity, ADD, cancer causing

Food or Food-Life Stuff	Known Symptoms From Consumption
Caffeine	Nervousness, insomnia, restlessness, anxiety
Low Carb Diets	Lack of energy, constipation, weakness, headaches, vitamin deficiencies, bone loss
Corn	Digestive Disease, bloating, indigestion, sluggishness
Dairy, Lactose, Whey	Aging, acne, chronic inflammation, digestive issues including IBS, diarrhea and bloating, bone loss, Mood swings, depression, respiratory problems like asthma or sinusitis?, itchy skin, eczema,
Soy	Intense menstrual cramps, hormonal acne, low thyroid
Gluten	Bloating, IBS, acid reflux, diarrhea, chronic constipation, migraines, headaches, joint pains or aches, brain fog, depression, anxiety, ADD or ADHD, low thyroid, eczema or acne
Nightshades	Irritable bowels, heartburn, nerve problems, joint pain, Arthritis, diarrhea, acid reflux, swelling in the joins

Table 1[18] This is just scratching the surface and we will uncover more craziness later on, but use this information as a tool to tune into Body Wisdom rather than treating this information as hard and fast rules on what to eat.

There are so many examples where we treat the symptoms and not the underlying cause of the issues. That is why taking a holistic and functional approach to health sets us up for a healthy life where we aren't dependent on drugs to get through the day and our health care costs stop at the farmers market. We get to experience living a life where we aren't constantly feeling like victims to our bodies, rather they are powerful tools helping us create the life we have always wanted.

Throughout this book I share with you all about holistic nutrition and how to cultivate your own unique Body Wisdom around what foods work for your body and which does not. Woven in are mindset shifts so you can break free from living in the *diet mentality* and disordered eating framework and so you can eat intuitively and stop pursing weight-loss in the name of health.

Chapter 3 ACTION STEPS:

Discovery #1: Think about your health right now in this moment. What symptoms are you experiencing that you think could be related to diet and lifestyle? Said another way, what are some of the things your body has been telling you that maybe you have been ignoring and not truly addressing the root cause of?

Discovery #2: Intuitively ask yourself what the potential culprits could be. Meaning which foods do you think are contributing to the symptoms and discomfort in our body? What lifestyle choices could be contributing like exercise, self-care or stress management?

4
SOUL AND SAD

"We are indeed much more than what we eat, but what we eat can nevertheless help us to be much more than what we are."

—Adelle Davis

N ow that you are a more tuned into your body as a system, let's explore how different types of food can impact the way that you show up in your life each day.

This chapter is not about creating food rules or learning which foods will make you gain or lose weight rather about learning to eat foods that will help you feel better in your body. When we look from the perspective of nourishing and healing our body, rather than shrinking them, the conversation around food changes entirely. Given the fact that as a society we are all so fat-phobic and all desperately want to be skinny, most conversations around food are about making sure we do not eat too much.

While we are pursuing health by monitoring our diets, we are simultaneously pursuing weight-loss through various tactics that almost always degrade our Body Wisdom. We will reduce calories, count points, and even track macros instead of honoring our bodies hunger and fullness signals. Sometimes we remove entire food groups, go fat free or carb free, or even purchase trendy supplements all in an effort to decrease our body size. When we shift our mindset from shrinking our bodies in the name of "health", to nourishing our bodies in the name of "health," the question changes from "am I eating too much" to "am I eating enough?"

Am I eating enough life-force giving foods to provide the vitamins, minerals, phytochemicals, fiber and hydration my body needs to thrive?

Am I eating enough leafy greens and vegetables to feed my gut bacteria and provide cell-protective antioxidants?

Am I eating enough healthy fat from avocados, nuts and seeds so my brain and cells can function?

Am I eating enough quality protein from pasture raised meat, eggs and beans so my body can build and repair my tissues?

I find that when we move weight-loss aside and focus on true health and nourishment we are so much more free to make empowered choices for ourselves around food. We no longer are in a scarcity mindset that often creates restriction and are now in an abundance mindset with so much more freedom and ease. This chapter is about these nourishing foods and foods that often do more harm than good for our body machines from biological standpoint. Chances are, you already know most of what I am about to share so if that's the case let it act as reassurance and a quick refresher.

Just keep in mind that this chapter is not meant to convince you that you can never eat "unhealthy" foods ever again. This chapter is designed to give you an idea of when a food provides true biological and physical nourishment, like a big vegetable salad as opposed to emotional nourishment, like cake on your birthday, which I talk about later on in this book.

So without further ado, let's get into SOUL + SAD food.

Everyone loves a good acronym: FOMO, FML, WTF, the list goes on.

Are you familiar with SOUL or SAD? They are definitely not your typical millennial slang and may not be in your vocabulary just yet, but get excited because these two words will help you categorize real food vs. food-like stuff in the easiest way possible.

SOUL FOOD

SOUL is an acronym I learned while studying nutrition and the simplicity of it struck me right away.[19] I knew it would be a tool I would use to help others determine what foods could be filling up their plates.

SOUL, which stands for **S**easonal, **O**rganic, **U**nprocessed, and **L**ocal, is the best framework to use when choosing how to eat and navigate the grocery store. It consists of minimally processed fresh and whole fruits, vegetables, grains, seeds, and legumes. It can include wild caught fish, organic pasture-raised animals and pastured eggs as well.

SEASONAL

Seasonal foods allow you to eat in sync with the earth and utilize nature's wisdom, which offers the types of food you will need during the different times of the year. It's not an accident that juicy and hydrating fruits and vegetables like cucumbers and watermelon are available in summer whereas more hearty and grounding squash, sweet potatoes, or pumpkins that require cooking are available in winter. Our nutritional needs vary during the different seasons so the food does as well.

Humans have been on this planet for hundreds of thousands of years and nature has provided all the foods we need to thrive.[20] The positives of eating in alignment with momma Earth means the food will taste better, be higher in nutrients, sprayed with less pesticides, cost less, and keep you more vibrant.

ORGANIC

Organic produce and other ingredients are grown without the use of conventional pesticides, synthetic fertilizers, sewage sludge, GMO (genetically modified organisms), or ionizing radiation[21] and studies show that this yields more nutritious food with higher antioxidant levels.[22] Also, organic animals are not given antibiotics or growth hormones. Although organic food can often be more expensive, *remember-* our health is an investment that pays dividends over time. Upfront, our groceries might cost us more when we focus on purchasing preventative SOUL food, but the upfront cost is exponentially less than the downstream potential costs of medical bills, prescriptions, and doctor's visits. If we spend less time sick, we can be more productive in other areas of our life. Organic foods are far better for the environment as well because the herbicides and pesticides used on conventional crops pollute groundwater, deplete soil of its vital nutrients and reduce biodiversity in the ecosystem surrounding the farm.[23] Plus organic food often tastes better in my experience.

UNPROCESSED

One of my favorite Michael Pollan quotes is "if it comes from a plant eat it, if it's made in a plant don't." While I don't think you have to avoid processed foods at all costs, eating unprocessed food most of the time has far reaching benefits. Unprocessed food will not be made in a plant because it is whole, made from the earth and served straight to your table. Anything that comes in a box, has a nutritional label or any kind of packaging is most likely processed to some degree. This of course is not considering cooking which is a form of processing. When choosing foods to nourish our bodies we want to focus on foods that are unprocessed or as minimally processed as possible. Essentially in as close to their original form. That doesn't mean that all foods from a package are unhealthy or need to be avoided. If you look at the nutritional label and can understand and identify all the ingredients then it is minimally processed and most likely a healthful option. The emphasis on eating unprocessed foods means we will most likely feel better in our body since these foods often balance our blood sugar and flood the body with vital nutrients.

LOCAL

Local food means the foods are grown and sold in the same region or state when you are purchasing them. I fully understand that not everyone lives in an agriculturally rich state like California, but even finding foods that are grown in the United States as opposed to overseas can have an impact on cost and nutritional value. Shopping at local farmers markets, participating in a CSA (Community Supported Agriculture), or ordering from Ugly Produce are some of the best ways to ensure you are getting high quality, locally grown foods. A quick Google search is all it takes to learn about what is available in your area.

Although SOUL foods can be more expensive depending on where you live in the United States, seasonal and local foods are often as affordable as conventional food that is out of season because they do not have to be packaged and shipped to make it to a store that is far away from where they are grown. And studies show that food loses its nutritional life force after harvest so the less time the food takes to make it to your plate means you will have more vitamin and mineral rich foods.[24] The less that is done to the food before it gets to your plate the better it likely is for your physical and biological health! This is why SOUL foods that are close to their unadulterated form as they are found in nature, is ideally the route to take as often as possible. These foods offer the highest nutrient content per calorie and were designed to feed you, all the way down to a cellular level.

Although science has uncovered the role that various nutrients play in the body, there is still much to be learned about how our body system processes nutrients. There are hundreds of compounds, vitamins, minerals and phytonutrients inside our food that go through a variety of mechanical, molecular and chemical changes in the body that we still don't fully understand. What we do know is that our current method of processing foods changes this and as we will discuss next, hasn't been good for the health of our bodies.

SAD FOOD

Humans have created some amazing and radical things; airplanes, the internet, Instagram, self-driving cars. Real cool shit if you ask me! But food… Americans don't always make the best food. And I don't mean cooking or baking. I mean creating food through mechanical, molecular or chemical processing. We engineer food-like stuff that really isn't food because it is not found in nature therefore our bodies often don't recognize it as such.

Humans have been processing food in some form, like fermentation, preserving and cooking for thousands of years, but commercial and modern food processing and refining is still in its infancy as it began only a little over a hundred years ago in the late 1800's, first with corn flakes by the Kellogg brothers and later in the 1950's, a major shift occurred and processed food as we know it today became the norm.[25] This modest beginning of an industry designed to provide convenience and accessibility to the American people has created what is now known as the Standard American Diet, or **SAD**, which consists predominantly of conventionally grown, highly refined food. These foods are some of the most advanced and sophisticated foods on the planet as millions of dollars has gone into creating the perfect balance of flavors making them irresistible. SAD foods include frozen meals, packaged foods, sodas, processed snacks, refined flour, Genetically Modified Organisms (GMOs) and fast food.

Not all processed and packaged food is unhealthy, in fact there are some great options these days (Whole Foods and Thrive Market carry awesome products) but the majority of these items are high in calories, stripped of fiber, full of simple carbohydrates, high fructose corn syrup, processed fats, added sugar, sodium, and chemicals. Most of these foods are not designed to be healthy or high in nutrients. Rather, their purpose is to provide convenience and an opportunity to save money upfront for both consumer and producer, but what saves us money on our grocery bill is costing us our health in the long run.

75% of the diseases killing us including heart disease, stroke, cancer and type 2 diabetes are largely preventable through a shift in diet and lifestyle.[26] Now people all around the world who have adopted the eating practices of Americans by importing and consuming our foods are living and dying from these diseases too.

I firmly believe that health comes in all different shapes and sizes and that weight is a poor indication of health, so while I am sharing about the implications of the SAD I am not talking about weight gain or weight loss. I am specifically describing the breakdown in our body's functioning, decrease in our immunity and an increase in diagnoses for diabetes and cardiovascular diseases as a result of a diet rich in processed foods.[27] The SAD contributes to health issues including various cancers, immune system dysfunctions, digestive disorders, Alzheimer's, brain fog, depression, heart and liver disease.[28] Not to mention, often just feeling like crap after eating these foods because they do not truly nourish our bodies and often leaving us sluggish and fatigued. If you are someone that is tired all the time, I encourage you to take a look at your food choices.

Obviously, enjoying some items that fall into this category is perfectly ok and even encouraged so that you do not feel restricted and crazy, but it's undebatable that they do not have much (if any) nutritional value and will most likely not make you feel really great in your body.

While these foods are often the cheapest available, they are truly costing us a lot in terms of our health when regularly consumed. Just think about the people you know for a minute. Your parents, siblings, aunts, uncles, grandparents and coworkers. How many of them are on medication for a chronic yet potentially preventable disease? These include type 2 diabetes, cancer, high blood pressure, heart disease and arthritis.[29] How about ADHD, depression, anxiety, acne, Alzheimer's or dementia (which is being called type 3 diabetes).

Crazy High Healthcare Costs

According to the CDC, 86% percent of the nation's $2.7 trillion annual healthcare costs are for people with chronic and mental health conditions.[29] What is more shocking is that according to the CDC, 85% of these conditions are from factors other than genetics.[30] (hint: that means diet and lifestyle.) So if we consider how much poor quality food impacts our health, the cost of eating these cheap SAD foods is quite steep.

If you are at all pissed about how much your healthcare costs you and your family, then look no further for an explanation. There is enough science and statistical data pointing to what we put in our bodies as one of the main reasons why healthcare is so expensive. Don't get me wrong, there is a lot of injustice happening like corporate greed at play as well, (which I will get to shortly) but we have to take responsibility and be accountable where we can.

The CDC collects data on where our health care dollars go and as previously mentioned the majority are spent on lifestyle related diseases. Below are some statistics from their reports:

- Between 2012-2013 cardiovascular disease cost the nation $316.1 billion
- Cancer care costs were $157 billion in 2010
- Diabetes costs were $245 billion in 2012
- In 2003, arthritis costs were $128 million

The impact of chronic illness is pervasive and it is now starting to affect people of all ages. 90% of Americans age 2 and older are consuming excessive amounts of sugar and sodium which can increase their risk for high blood pressure, diabetes and metabolic syndrome.[31] We are now seeing children as young as 3 develop Type 2 Diabetes which used to only affect the older population and be called "adult onset diabetes."[32] When we consider the relationship between eating a nutrient-depleted diet and the ever increasing prevalence of chronic illness, it becomes obvious why our health care dollars are being poured into disease management. The food industry and our government policy is not completely responsible, as there is another side to the story that is sometimes overlooked.

Lack of Price Transparency In Our Healthcare System

Consumers will usually invest their time to shop based on price comparison for most of life's essentials ranging from lower expense basics such as groceries all the way to higher ticket items such as a car. Yet when it comes to healthcare procedures, consumers can't utilize their savvy shopper skills to the same degree and often have to invest their trust (and welfare) in the medical system to direct them to the "best" service.

When our primary care doctor tells us to get a colonoscopy or a blood test we generally will go to where they refer us instead of looking for the best quality service at the most affordable price. Our medical system is the only industry that makes "shopping around" incredibly difficult for the consumer. Furthermore, it is the only industry that does not make it easy to obtain complete and accurate information on what and where we will spend our healthcare dollars. There is almost no price transparency.

Since consumers are left in the dark about what various procedures and referrals will cost, companies including insurance agencies, hospitals and doctor's offices have no incentive to price their services competitively to earn your business. Often there are agreements between care providers and insurance agencies so you don't have a choice anyways. Price transparency and a more free market could greatly disrupt the way health care is bought in this country and potentially lead to better care at a lower price.

While we might feel powerless against the entire system because there are many things out of our control when it comes to the cost of food and health care, we cannot let ourselves become victims. Blaming everything on outside influences and circumstances takes away our personal power and responsibility over our lives.

Many of us have the ability to choose what we eat and that choice is a form of voting with our wallets. That said, I want to bring attention to the fact that while this chapter focuses on the physiological and environmental impact of different foods, it does not necessarily address the socio-economic disadvantages that some populations of Americans face with regard to food availability. Unfortunately, fresh, organic, and minimally processed foods are more expensive as a result of many issues within our food and farming industry (which we will get into later). While social justice issues surrounding food availability and affordability are incredibly significant, the purpose of this book is to focus on the power of choice within the individual who is seeking to heal their relationship with food and develop food intuition through cultivating their Body Wisdom.

If food availability or accessibility is something you regularly struggle with, this chapter is by no means intended to instill a sense of guilt, shame, or embarrassment. If you are able to apply the principles of SOUL food into your lifestyle in a way that is economically possible, I hope this chapter provides useful information on how you can do so. When we are able to choose not to be victims of the system and instead take responsibility for our own health, we discover how to feel empowered by this knowledge and use it to make informed choices whenever possible.

By focusing on what we do have the ability to change, we can discover where our food freedom lies, which is why having an understanding of how different foods make us feel is so powerful. Ultimately, we can choose to feel vibrant or we can choose to feel depleted based on the quality of the food we eat and the information we ingest.

Shifting your Priorities to Shift your Health

When health and nourishment becomes our priority, we will move and shift things we previously thought were impossible to change. For me, feeling sick all the time, being victim to arbitrary numbers like weight, and poor body image were eating my spirit alive so I committed myself to honoring my body and truly nourishing it with SOUL food.

Of course, I am not saying that you should create food rules where you can only eat this and must avoid that. Rather I want to highlight and express the importance and the power of healing foods. When we fuel ourselves with foods that make us feel good, all areas of our life can shift and it is truly an expression of love for our bodies which is a form of self-care and in turn self-love- both of which in my experience are truly life changing.

By eating SOUL-fully our mood can lift, we can be more energized, creative, sleep better, have better digestion and so on..., all these improvements will affect every facet of life from relationships, body-acceptance, work, you name it. It's not about going on another restrictive diet, rather shifting the focus from losing weight or having the perfect body to truly nourishing ourselves.

Fundamentally, healing our relationship with food and discovering Body Wisdom begins by deciding that we want true wellbeing, peace of mind, sanity and food freedom more than we want anything else we have previously been prioritizing and chasing after. And based on my own experience and the experience of many of my clients, connecting and getting present to how healthier whole foods make us feel in our bodies is unbelievably powerful. This is why I truly believe getting as much SOUL food as you can is an important part of this journey.

My hope is that you understand that what we eat truly matters and later in this book I will help you uncover how to eat and how to think about food so you can have an amazing relationship with it.

Chapter 4 ACTION STEPS:

Discovery #1 Think about what you have eaten today and if possible, yesterday. How much of it was SOUL food and how much of it was SAD food? Are you able to decipher how various foods make you feel?

Discovery #2: How much of the information in this last chapter were you already aware off? Do you feel like you know a lot of what I just mentioned, but sometimes still struggle to make choices that honor your body? I am asking this because what I have found is that the majority of us already know a lot about nutrition and healthful food but the way we think about food and eating is often where we get stuck.

Our mindset is what needs a makeover, so sit tight and we will get to it later on.

5
HEALTH OR MARKETING

"Asking the Department of Agriculture to promote healthy eating was like asking Jack Daniels to promote responsible drinking"

—Denise Minger

N ow that you know the difference between real food and food-like stuff, which I sometimes call play-food, let's dive into how to further decipher what factors impact your decisions on what to eat. This chapter is meant to help you trust your intuition more by explaining that we can't always trust everything we are told by the health food industry. One of the best things we can do for ourselves in our pursuit of Body Wisdom is to develop "media literacy" and become an educated consumer who is less vulnerable to clever marketing tactics used to either create fear or sell products. Given our modern landscape of news, media and access to information, it's crucial that we question all headlines and health claims.

News Headlines and Health Claims

Each day the average American will see between 4,000 to 10,000 different ads and marketing messages.[33] With this abundance of information and opinions confronting us on the daily, it can be challenging to decipher what is relevant and true for our health. When we delve into the resources available designed to "help" us make conscious decisions on how to eat healthy, it can be like walking into a dodgeball game where players from each team are fighting tooth and nail to win you over.

Everywhere you turn there are balls in the form of facts, statistics and studies showing correlation or causation. This leads to attention grabbing headlines that can create fear or confusion in order to persuade us to purchase certain types of foods.

"Don't Eat This Food!"
"If You're Not Eating This You're Missing Out"
"New Study Shows XYZ Can Cause Cancer"
"Avoid These 10 Foods if you Want to Lose Weight".

It can be enough to make anyone's head spin and make you feel utterly confused on how to do something like feed yourself which should just be intrinsically simple.

To make matters worse, large corporations and industry insiders take advantage of the fact that purchasing food is essential for your survival and add manipulative language to health food claims in order to drive sales and profit. This results in a slew of conflicting articles and published studies that contradict each other or challenge what were once popularly held beliefs. Whether science backed or not, there is a ton of statistical and anecdotal information from a variety of sources, so it's hard to know who to trust and understand what will work for your body. We live in a world where anyone can write anything on the internet and conflicts of interest are the norm.

For example, in June of 2017 an article was published on USAtoday. com that was based on information from the American Heart Association (AHA) that referenced old studies published in the 1960's about how coconut oil and saturated fat lead to heart disease. One of the main attention grabbing headlines said "Coconut Oil Isn't Healthy and It's Never Been Healthy[34] ". Yet there is support from many leading health and wellness experts that recommend coconut oil as an excellent oil choice for cooking, as a DIY moisturizer, and even as an aid for maintaining a healthy weight for your body because it supports the feelings of satiety.

The recoil of this coconut oil-bashing article sent the interwebs into a major tizzy and I, like many other healthy living experts, were bombarded with emails, texts and DM's asking our opinion about it. The American Heart Association re-released dietary guidelines in response to this article telling Americans to eat more heavily processed vegetable and seed oils such as canola and rapeseed oil, but to avoid other oils like coconut oil.[35] What's maddening is that there is a plethora of documented research that supports how vegetable and seed oils contribute to excess inflammation in the body. Inflammation has been touted as the root cause of most chronic health conditions in our country, so the fact that foods that are linked to excess inflammation are being recommended by one of our most esteemed governing bodies in the United States makes us seriously question why these counter-intuitive recommendations are being made. And to be frank, the abuse of power pisses me off immensely.

Crop Subsidies and Corrupt Dietary Recommendations

If we evaluate the subsidies made by our government for specific crops we will find that vegetable and seed oils are cheap to make, and are a major agricultural commodity of the Big Farming Industry in America. The fact that the dietary guidelines that come from the United States Department of Agriculture (USDA) include these processed seed oils indicates how intertwined major money making crops like seeds are with sales tactics such as the USDA recommendations. If you don't think that the recommendations will be biased in an effort to protect and promote agriculture, think again. Just follow the money.

This makes us question how the major crop industries that support the overproduction of cheap and processed foods such as GMO-soybean, corn, canola, etc. are interrelated with the dietary recommendations made by the government. If nationwide recommendations are being made that are contradictory to what the most recent scientific research says about the foods that lead to chronic disease, what does that say about the reliability of government proposed dietary recommendations for our country?

Unfortunately for the propaganda of the AHA, millions of people, myself included, have felt the positive effects of adding undamaged saturated fats into our diet. It has helped balance my hormones, keeps me feeling satiated, increases my energy and also my ability to focus. Hello, Brain Octane by Bulletproof, MCT and coconut oil in coffee anyone?

Maybe you have experienced benefits too, but weren't fully present to your body's signals so you may have let your mind, and this campaign against coconut oil and saturated fat, sway your opinion on what to eat. If you find yourself questioning if the USDA dietary recommendations will actually help you to feel your best, this book is designed to help you eliminate this concern. The essence of this book is to set you up to trust what your body tells you while not allowing the outside world to decide for you. Yet, until we have a strong connection to our body, it can be hard to tune out the ever changing news cycle.

Just Another PR Stunt

Learning to trust your body is the most reliable source you will ever have as sadly, even the largest and most "reputable" organizations use propaganda and PR stunts to sway your food choices to drive sales and profit for the Big Food industries in America. Unfortunately, the recommendation to avoid coconut oil and other natural sources of saturated fats turned out to be an orchestrated PR stunt by the AHA to benefit its corporate sponsors. Furthermore, humans have been eating saturated fat for as long as they have been on this planet because it is richly found in animals and some plants! The same cannot be said for processed vegetable oils like canola or soybean oils. This is just one example of how our governing bodies choose to disregard what recent research suggests about the importance of healthy fats in our diets, and instead support lobbyist for Big Food.

What is extra infuriating is that the marketing director who lead the campaign used to be an executive at KFC and other fast food chains. [36] Unfortunately, this type of revolving door is a regular thing between big regulatory agencies, Big Agriculture, Big Pharma and Big Food companies. Ultimately, it is a conflict of interest that puts industry profit before the health of our country. And if you are not convinced that the consumers' health is secondary, I encourage you to consider the fact that one of the corporate sponsors of the AHA is The Canola Oil Council who would directly benefit from the opinion that coconut oil is dangerous for your health. [37] The article that bashed coconut oil appeared to be smear campaign to sway consumers to eat more of the processed and heart-damaging "food" created by the Big Food industry so that they could sell more products that are high in refined vegetable oils and sugar. If you need more proof that non-profit bodies such as the AHA are often corrupt due to their relationship with Big Food and Big Farming, just check out some of the products at your grocery store that tout the AHA's "Heart Check Mark" logo. Most of these products are low-in fat, high in sugar, and contain inflammatory vegetable and seed oils, all of which have been scientifically proven to be harmful for our body machines, especially when consumed in excess. From my own experience, many of these products make me feel physically lousy after I eat them so it's hard for me to believe that they are actually good for my heart.

There are several products that are eligible for that seal that are at this point irrefutably unhealthy, including some cereals, canned soups, yogurt, crackers, pancakes, muffins and breads with added sugar and corn syrup. Processed and refined foods are far from what nature had intended us to eat and it's indisputable that these foods contribute to insulin resistance, inflammation and chronic illness, like heart disease, cancer and diabetes especially when eaten in excess. I will dive further into the corruption of our food system later on and how it helped me heal my relationship with my food and body.

Luckily the internet and social media makes it hard for this type of false information to permeate like it once did. We have access to medical journals and studies so we can read the science ourselves and come to our own conclusions. Plus, no one else but us can tell how we feel after we eat certain foods. I eat more forms of healthy fat than ever before and I have also never felt better in my body- to me that is all the information I need. Forget all that fat-free bullshit- eating healthy fat from real foods has truly made a difference in how I feel each day.

This is just one more reason why it is more important than ever to trust your body when making food choices and be skeptical of information from biased sources. Like grocery stores, food companies create products to sell because they are a business. So the next time you find yourself reaching for foods that are packaged, it's wise to check out the ingredient label and be sure to question whether the health claims on the front are a clear representation of how the "food" inside will impact your health and body.

Given the amount of contradictory information at our fingertips and controversial marketing like the Coconut Oil vs Canola Oil example, it's easy to understand why we get confused and do not know where to start. So many new processed foods have been introduced into our society that are being shown to have detrimental effects, yet as we uncovered with the example of the AHA, many of these products were never designed to be consumed in amounts they are today. As Michael Pollan said, "the way we eat has changed more in the last 50 years then in the previous 10,000."[38] Most of our human history was spent searching for enough food to survive each year, but now most modern humans have so much abundance and options for food that it's difficult to determine what choices to make.

But I believe it's actually *very, very simple*. The best place to start is to look to nature. If nature made it, great! If a human made it, proceed with awareness.

Nutritional Labels

Although possible, it would be difficult to eat 100% whole SOUL foods that we cook all of the time, so learning how to read nutritional labels and understanding the difference between a food that naturally has nutrients versus a food (or food-like product) that has been fortified with nutrients will help you make the most nutritive choice possible. Ultimately, this will arm you with the ability to decipher what is healthy versus what is just good old marketing.

Nature, over hundreds of thousands of years, has created food that humans are designed to eat. It has assembled vitamins, minerals, phytonutrients, macronutrients, fiber, flavors, and textures together to create edible things that our bodies benefit from, recognize as food, and help us thrive. Nature is smart such that it has created food in a way that our bodies know what to do with it. These whole foods have one ingredient, like a cucumber, avocado or chicken and these are the types of foods that will help balance blood sugar, support brain function, and decrease our risk for chronic illness. Not to mention, they just have a higher vibration that will increase our life force energy because they are living foods.

Processed food created by humans doesn't have that kind of wisdom woven into it and is generally combined with preservatives, additives, chemicals, sweeteners, food coloring, low quality fat, tons of sugar and refined flours. They do not elicit the same hormonal response as whole foods do so we are less likely to feel full and satiated which is why we tend to eat past the point of fullness with processed foods. There isn't really an off button inside our bodies. Our body doesn't treat them the same because they are not the same. A processed food is anything with more than one ingredient in it and it changes the food from something that our body can easily recognize and metabolize. Unfortunately, our body does not always respond to processed foods as foods.

A great example is a baked potato (one ingredient) compared to instant mashed potatoes. The ingredients list for Hungry Jack instant mash is the following:

Idaho Potato Flakes (sodium acid, pyrophosphate, sodium bisulfite, BHA and citric acid added to protect color and flavor), contains 2% or less of vegetable monoglyceride, hydrogenated cottonseed oil and natural flavor. Contains Milk.

With all of these added ingredients and chemicals plus the processed oils, I have to ask...is this even real food anymore? My response is no, it's *food-like.* And I am not surprised at all that our body does not fully know how to metabolize and process it.

If you go to any supermarket and look at the items on the shelf you will see products that make all kinds of health claims. Everything from low-fat, low-sugar, low-sodium, reduced guilt, gluten-free, heart healthy, great source of calcium, enriched with XYZ, natural, organic and on... and on...and on.

How Sugar and Artificial Ingredients Replaced Fiber and Fat

So many of these products have been manipulated in a lab to extend their shelf life and increase profitability. One way is by striping the whole ingredient of its fiber and using this refined version in the product. While this might benefit the manufacture, it does not have many benefits for the human body. Fiber is necessary to support healthy digestion, healthy blood cholesterol, decrease our chance of becoming diabetic and slow the absorption of sugar, thus controlling our insulin response.[39] Fiber also helps keep you feeling satiated and discourages continuous consumption. According to the Institute for Medicine, Americans are getting less than half the recommended daily amount of fiber which directly contributes to the growth of our waistlines and deficits in our health.[40] Another nutrient that food companies removed from their products is fat. Back in 1958, a prominent researcher by the name of Ancel Keys began to explore the link between dietary fat, cholesterol and coronary heart disease. He hypothesized that there was a direct link between these factors, and ultimately set out to prove himself right.

His original data collected included information from 22 countries and when combing through the research he found that the link between dietary fat, cholesterol and coronary heart disease was not very distinct. In fact there was no definitive link at all. Instead of being transparent and thorough with his research, Keys manipulated the information by publishing data collected from only seven of the 22 countries, and thus released his *Seven Countries Study*. By cherry picking the data to support his hypothesis instead of the actual results, he wrongly influenced the world and dietary recommendations by our government and medical system to remove fat from our diet.[40] This lead to the fat-free craze of the 80's and 90's and since everyone wanted to avoid heart disease, food companies started creating a low-fat or fat-free version of all our favorite food products to turn a profit. By removing fat from food, many things became tasteless so manufactures "corrected" this issue with palatability by increasing the sugar content to keep their products desirable to consumers. We started to see everything from puddings to bread to cookies to yogurt to meat products being marketed as "healthier" options because they were low in fat. Consequently, people would choose a Snack Well cookie over a beautiful avocado because we were all afraid of fat and told it was the more healthful option.

This ended up being detrimental to our health because we were over-consuming processed *food-like* products that were high in simple carbohydrates, added sugars, low in fat and devoid of fiber. This was a recipe for disaster as these *food-ish* things spike the body's blood sugar and produce an inflammatory metabolic response where too much insulin is produced. Excess insulin from perpetual spikes in blood sugar has been linked to countless chronic health conditions such as insulin resistance and diabetes.(42) Plus it makes us feel lousy, fatigued and irritable which is no fun at all.

Metabolism Crash Course

As a quick metabolism background, *Insulin* is the hormone our pancreas produces that allows the body to use glucose for energy by pulling it into our cells. Without insulin, the body experiences chronically high levels of blood sugar (glucose) which is inflammatory and can damage the body. Those with Type I diabetes are born with a pancreas that is unable to produce insulin, hence their requirement to inject insulin whenever they eat a meal with carbohydrate.

Glucose is the first form of energy that will be used by the body because it is the most easily metabolized and broken down. It is the end product of a string of metabolic processes that transforms carbohydrate from starchy vegetables, fruit, table sugar, bread, beans, and grains into a usable form of energy for the body. So when we eat these forms of sugar, the pancreas is required to produce insulin to keep our blood sugar levels in a balanced range preventing it from getting to low (hypoglycemia) or too high (hyperglycemia).[43] Our country regularly consumes processed foods, ingest too much sugar or refined flour that turns into sugar, too quickly and too often. When our blood sugar is continually being spiked over time from our consumption of these foods, our pancreas is constantly producing insulin. Eventually inflammation from excess blood sugar can not only damage our pancreas making it unable to produce sufficient insulin, but the cells of our body become lazy to the effects of insulin, or *insulin resistant*. Insulin resistance is a condition where our bodies no longer respond to the effects of insulin, which can play a role in the development of diabetes, and potentially heart disease.[44] Our body was not designed to have a steady flow of sugar in the system without fiber being present to slow down the digestion and metabolism.

What's compounding this issue is that food companies are clever and have found new ways of incorporating sugar into processed foods to accomplish their goal of selling products that make them money, but damage our health in the long run. And part of this processing means there is no "off button" in terms of feeling satisfied which leads to overconsumption and endless cravings.

Unfortunately, manufacturers of food don't just list sugar as sugar because that would be too obvious. Rather the food industry has renamed and rebranded sugar so that it can be listed under the names of various additives, which ultimately makes it harder for you to decipher exactly what it is that you are ingesting into your beautiful body machine.

On the next page is a list of the different ways sugar can be labeled.

Sugar AKA:

Agave	Dextrose	Invert sugar	Refiner's syrup
Barley malt	Evaporated cane juice	Maltodextrin	Rice syrup
Beet sugar	Evaporated cane sugar	Maltose	Rice syrup solids
Cane sugar	Fructose	Maple syrup	Sorghum syrup
cornstarch	Fruit juice concentrates	Modified corn starch	sucrose
Corn syrup	Glucose	Molasses	Sugar
Corn syrup solids	honey	Organic cane sugar	Turbinado sugar
Crystalline fructose	High fructose corn syrup	Raw sugar	

It's **all** sugar.

While this is not a push to never eat sugar again, because restriction can lead to binge eating and feelings of deprivation, we instead want to bring awareness to the fact that processed foods are not natural for our body and often make us feel like crap. I eat processed foods from time to time, I truthfully do. I am not an "all or nothing" type of girl, but I see value in knowing how these foods affect our body because it helps me become more aware to how I feel after eating them which was truly helpful on my road to recovery. It played a role in shifting my perspective from eating for weight loss *in the name of health* to truly eating for longevity and vibrancy. I started to truly value my body and I wanted to feel good which meant paying attention to the signals it sent me after eating certain things.

Sugar is available to us in nature, so I truly believe it's ok to eat it in moderate amounts. However, natural sugar that is present in nature is presented much differently than the sugar found in processed foods that flood the modern world. Natural sugar in fruit, aka "nature's candy", is packaged with fiber, vitamins, and complex carbohydrates that all positively impact the body. Even sugar cane, which is one of the primary sources of added sugar, is in its raw form as an insanely fibrous plant bark. The industrial processing of natural sugar has resulted in highly concentrated forms that are extremely unnatural. There is nothing in nature that resembles a candy bar, muffin or a can of soda, even if it's "diet."

Luckily, the new food labeling law requires companies to list the added sugars in the food whereas before the naturally occurring sugars and added sugars were clumped together. Food companies had to comply with the new law by Summer 2018. If you are going to eat a packaged food product, look for ones with as few ingredients as possible, that you can recognize, that also has fiber and little to no added sugar.

While it is important to make sure we pay attention to the amount of added sugars in food, we still want to be sure to keep in mind that there are foods that turn into sugar in the body. In fact nearly every wheat product on the supermarket shelf are made with enriched flour which is a highly processed version of wheat that metabolizes into sugar very quickly in the body.

To get a whole wheat berry into a form that is commonly found in packaged bread, food processors remove the bran and the germ of the seed which is where the fiber, protein, trace minerals, healthy fats, and B vitamins are found. Essentially the nutrients that nature intended for us to eat when eating wheat are stripped away, thus extending the shelf life but degrading the nutritional benefits of the wheat.

Then the flour is chemically bleached and we are left with cheap white flour that does not resemble anything close to "wheat" and instead leaves us nutritionally deficient of all the goodness nature originally intended us to ingest. In the 1940's our government attempted to combat these deficiencies by enriching the heavily processed flour with B vitamins, calcium, and iron in an effort to restore the quality and nutritional value of the flour.

Although this might seem like a good thing, enriching a heavily processed wheat flour does not restore the grain back to how nature created and it does not address the lack of fiber, which is crucial for the body to have available when eating carbohydrates. Unfortunately, science does not fully understand all the molecular and chemical processes that take place in our bodies during the digestion and absorption of food. There are valuable phytonutrients inside food along with vitamins and minerals in quantities that your body is familiar with and needs for a healthy metabolism.

The prevalence of nutrient deficiencies in our country tends to raise concern for many health-conscious people, and leads them to question whether supplementation is right for them. What many people do not realize is that getting nutrition from SOUL foods is far superior to getting our nutrition from packaged and shelf-stable lab-created nutrients.

When you take a supplement or eat an enriched product, you are getting highly concentrated mega-dose of nutrients. Additionally, there are compounds called cofactors that are packaged with nutrients found in food that may or may not be included in the supplement formulation. Have you ever heard of fat soluble vitamins? This refers to certain vitamins that can only be absorbed in the body when dietary fat is present, so consuming these nutrients without fat guarantees that these nutrients will be poorly absorbed, if they are absorbed at all.

These are the types of processes taking place in the body when we eat whole foods, many of which are not taken into consideration when developing products for sale. But from what we do know, fortification and supplementation is not as effective or beneficial compared to eating whole foods. Although supplements can *supplement* a healthy diet and be very therapeutic at times, there is no way to supplement your way out of poor eating.

Although, I do not advocate for processed foods for many reasons, I get that avoiding them one hundred percent of the time is unrealistic. Even I eat them sometimes because I never want to feel restricted. That said, below are the guidelines I use when choosing a processed and packaged food:

1. If you can't pronounce an ingredient yourself then it is most likely that your body won't recognize it either.
2. Choose products with as few ingredients as possible
3. Skip the artificial food colorings if possible
4. Skip products made with artificial sweeteners if possible
5. Be curious about any health claim made on the front of a product packaging. Read the ingredients and decide for yourself.
6. If you do eat SAD food, truly enjoy it and do not feel guilty- you gotta live your life and receive pleasure from all foods!

Chapter 5 ACTION STEPS:

Discovery #1: Think about the last time an attention grabbing headline influenced your decision on whether or not to eat something. What was the claim and do you still believe it. If not, how has your opinion changed since?

Discovery #2: What types of health claims on packages influence your buying decisions? For example: vegan, low fat, gluten free, guilt free etc. Why do these influence your buying decision? What fears or ideas do you have around these types of nutrients or claims?

6

YOUR SECOND BRAIN

"If you want to fix your health, start with your gut. Gut health literally affects your entire body."

—Dr. Mark Hyman

Now that we have discussed the food available to us and how it's sold and marketed to us, we are going to get into one of my favorite topics about how food can truly impact who we are as humans.

Often we hear about the mind-body connection where what we think and feel can have a physiological impact on the body. Nike's "Just do it" slogan is a commercialized example of feeling resistance in the body but using mental tenacity to *will* the body into action. Beyond the ability to use this mind-body connection to sell sportswear, this unseen ability that we possess has been scientifically researched and proven legitimate. Perhaps the most notable example of the mind-body connection is the placebo effect.

The placebo effect is one example where the power of the mind can convince the body that sugar pills (placebo) are as powerful as Prozac,[45] fake surgeries are as effective as actual surgeries,[46] and non-alcoholic drinks are in fact intoxicating. The effectiveness of a placebo boils down to the psychological belief and expectation that something will have a biological effect on the body. In instances where a placebo is as effective as actual treatment, this exhibits how belief can produce physiological changes within the body. "What you think you become" as the Buddha so notably said. Even stress plays a critical role in the development of diseases. What is less well-known and studied is the profound influence the body and its inhabitants can have on the mind or well, our brain and health as a whole.

Into the Wilderness

Inside each of our bodies is a "vast, largely uncharted internal wilderness", as Michael Pollan puts it.[47] You may have heard about the "gut microbiome" before this book and how the bacteria in our digestive system literally communicate with our entire body, which makes the mind-body connection even more intricate. Scientist have just started to explore the garden of gut bugs we share our bodies with. These microscopic creatures are part of an interdependent ecosystem of living organisms known as bacteria and create our somewhat mysterious gut-microbiome.

This diverse colony consists of some 500–1000 species and accounts for about 3-6 pounds of physical matter.[48] What is most intriguing about these little guys is that their DNA out numbers our human DNA 10:1. For every human cell in our body, we have 10 resident microbes. More simply put, just looking at the numbers alone, we are in fact only 10% human and 90% bacteria.[49] That is nothing short of mind boggling and leads me to wonder why nature had us designed this way.

The food we eat is indistinguishably linked to health of our microbial inhabitants and as a result, our health as well. Irregularities in our bacteria, like a lack of diversity, or the proliferation of "bad" bacteria, can lead to a weakened immune system, mood disorders, weight gain and other more serious chronic health issues. Several studies have found that the gut bacteria of thin mice transplanted into the gut of obese mice improves their metabolic syndrome symptoms and causes them to lose weight.[50] In essence, the amount, diversity, and strains of bacteria in our gut can influence our physical and mental health. The richness of the colonies living inside us is without a doubt massively influential in our personal health, but science is still uncovering how and why it all works this way.

While the genes we inherit from our parents are for the most part fixed, it's slowly becoming apparent that we can transform and cultivate the collection of bacterial genes in our microbiome. We now know that these little bugs play a huge role in regulating our immune system by determining what is an "invader" and what is a "peacekeeper." The way in which the body reacts to offending foods we ingest (like nuts, gluten or eggs) or to unintentional exposure to pathogens or viruses, is a direct result of the opinions of our internal peanut gallery. The exponential rise of autoimmune diseases is arguably linked to a decrease in the health of our gut microbiome and a result of the processed foods we are regularly consuming, aka SAD foods. [51] Growing up we were taught that bacteria was this bad thing that needed to be avoided. Antibacterial soap and hand sanitizer is the norm in classrooms and antibiotics are widely overprescribed, but this growing understanding of the importance of preserving the health of our microbiome has begun to shift how we view bacteria. Although it is still unclear if gut bugs hold the cure to diseases that plague modern humans, the implications of what has been discovered has altered our interpretation of bacteria, our health, and what it means to look at the body as a whole. Based on the mounting evidence that our body functions through a systems approach, it's imperative that we avoid observing our beautiful body machine as a compilation of individual parts as we've previously discussed, but rather as a vibrant interconnected system of living organisms that all communicate with and influence each other.

How the Gut Microbiome Gets Colonized

In alliance with this holistic approach that we must adopt in order to treat the body as an ecological system, it is imperative that we understand how the gut microbiome is established and how we can live our lives to maintain a diverse and robust bacterial colony. The diversity, strength, and health of our gut microbiome is largely determined by the gut microbiome of our mother, from whom we gain our unique colony of bacteria during the first few months of our life. The colonization of our gut begins in utero but is largely established at birth, when the infant is exposed to the microbes present in the birthing canal and on the mother's skin during breastfeeding. Additional microbes are then passed from mother to baby through the actual breast milk, which is rich in probiotics and prebiotics to establish a strong bacterial colony in the baby's digestive tract.

There are a few factors that occur within the first few months of life that can reduce the health and diversity of the infant's gut microbiome. For example, babies born by Cesarean (C-section), a somewhat sterile procedure, are not exposed to the same vaginal and intestinal microbes as their vaginal birth counterparts.[52] Additionally, babies who are bottle fed might not have received all the same prebiotic -- food for the gut bugs, and probiotic --good bacteria for the gut, as those that were breastfed. As we begin to grow and explore the world more by getting our hands dirty, we are exposed to more bacteria which up until recently, was seen as a potentially harmful thing. Now we know more exposure to microbial diversity during the first months of our life improves the diversity of our gut microbiome and strengthens our immune system. While we are still very much in the early phases of uncovering the purpose, importance, and role of the gut in our overall health, we do recognize how important maintaining a healthy digestive system is for improving our well-being, preventing dis-ease and developing Body Wisdom.

While we are still learning about all of the functions our gut microbiome has in determining the status of our health, our understanding of the sheer inventory of favors our bacterial friends do for us is continuing to grow every day. Our microbial friends work hard to maintain our immune system by protecting us from pathogens, toxins, and bacterial invaders. For example, the robustness of one person's gut microbiome could explain why they don't fall victim to food poisoning while another person might after eating the same meal.

In addition to this protective ability, the gut plays a huge role in ensuring that we are extracting all the nutrition from our food. Not only does the gut microbiome help us assimilate nutrients from the food we eat, but it also manufactures a variety of substances like neurotransmitters, including dopamine and serotonin,[53] vitamins like B's and K, essential nutrients and a slew of signaling molecules that communicate with our immune and metabolic systems.

As a result of the role our gut microbiome plays in increasing the availability of nutrients from our food and synthesizing neurotransmitters, we have discovered that these bugs also play a role in our stress response and mood which is why it's an important aspect in developing a really strong connection to our body and our relationship to food.

The effects that the gut microbiome has on the stress response and mood state was observed by researchers from McMaster University who conducted an experiment with mice that had very different personalities such that some mice were adventurous, while others were very timid. They discovered that when the gut microbiome from the adventurous mice was removed and implanted into the digestive system of the timid mice, the personality of the latter became much more adventurous.[54] This alludes to the influence our gut has not only on our personality traits, but also makes us question if the saying of "trusting your gut instincts" can be supported scientifically.

Gut Instincts and the Gut Brain Connection

Scientifically proving the impact our gut bugs have on our overall health and personality gives more than a shred of truth to the idea of "trusting your gut." As I mentioned earlier, we now know that the "vagus nerve" serves as a primary connection between our brain and our gut. This connection serves as a bi-directional highway of constant communication between the brain and the gut, which makes the relationship between neurons, chemical messengers, hormones, and the gut-brain connection anything but metaphorical. For example, we might have a "gut-feeling" when we first meet someone, or decide to "trust our gut" when making an important decision. You know that pit in your stomach that you feel before public speaking or when you find out bad news, like failing a test or learning that your partner cheated on you? You become immediately stressed and your gut bugs know it. You might even feel sick to your stomach, or have "butterflies." This is tangible proof of a very real phenomenon going on inside our body. I know from personal experience, that by transitioning to eating predominately whole foods over time, has resulted in changes in my gut bacteria and a stronger connection to my intuition or gut instincts. The ability to listen or make decisions based on a gut-feeling has dramatically increased with a shift in how, when and what I eat which has also developed my Body Wisdom.

Interestingly, there are a similar number of neurons in our gut as there are in our spinal cord, which might seem excessive if we simply view the gut as a way to break down our food. [55] The ability for the gut to signal to the body, communicate to the brain through neurons, and impact our metabolism has earned the gut the nickname as the "second brain." Despite the insane discovery that the gut is nearly as intricate as the brain, it begs the questions of why we would even have a "second brain" in the digestive system anyways? While there is no short answer to that question, the incredible signaling ability of the gut microbiome has intrigued the scientific community and researchers have begun to evaluate the role our gut bacteria can play in all disease states including mood disorders like depression and anxiety, and behavioral disorders like autism.

Since the 1960's more than 150 scientific papers have been published on a link between gut bacteria and the Autism Spectrum Disorder. [56] The present research paints a pretty clear picture of the role that healthy bacteria play in decreasing the symptoms of autism. The initial development of autism can be from a number of factors that can be related to gut health such as how a baby was born, how long it was breastfed, the health of the mother, and the use of antibiotics with the child at a young age.[57] While more research is needed to verify this connection, the impact of the gut microbiome on disorders such as autism only supports the need to apply food as medicine to strengthen the compromised gut microbiome. Doctors who reviewed the present research on the connection between the gut microbiome and autism have tested this theory in small trials.[58] They found that changing the diet of those with autism by including probiotics and prebiotic foods and removing gluten and casein, resulted in a healthier gut and a change in behavior. While this is not a "cure all" for autism, it is very exciting research and again only reinforces the power of healing food and the importance of gut health in overall well-being.

The ability for food to be used as medicine in cases such as autism makes us question how we can apply these concepts to our everyday lives. According to the findings from The American Gut Project, the more variety of plants a person eats, the more diverse their gut bacteria is. Conversely, the more antibiotics a person is exposed to, the less healthy their gut is.[59] This tells us that our immune system benefits from nurturing the life of microbes by feeding them a diet rich in fibrous vegetables and SOUL-food and avoiding harmful compounds that destroy the microbiome such as antibacterial and antimicrobial agents as much as possible. Unfortunately antibiotics don't distinguish between friend or foe once they are in the digestive system, but rather wipes out all gut bugs in its path (it's important to emphasize that this is by no means a suggestion to stop taking antibiotics when medically necessary, be sure to consult your doctor. It is however, worth noting).

Exposing ourselves to bacteria and understanding that not all are harmful is a shift that is slowly occurring in the world of health. Some microbiologists and functional medicine doctors have been warning us about the destruction of the human microbiome and the fallout of the war on bacteria. There is no doubt that antibiotics have been beneficial and have helped extend our life expectancy, but with any war there are unintended consequences.

We have seen an epidemic rise of chronic illness and digestive disease. Some scientists say that our obsession with being "hyper-hygienic" and limiting our exposure to bacteria could also be contributing to the rise of Alzheimer's and Dementia, too.[60] The correlation between the sterile developing world and the rise of these diseases is not isolated causation. There are several factors of course, not all of which are concrete, that are affecting the robustness of our immune system by decreasing the health and versatility of our microbiome.

Could there be a link between specific bacterial strains and the health of the Western world? It's possible, and it is a question that a lot of scientists are now asking and seeking to answer. Since we now know that the immune system in housed in our gut, it makes sense that to help heal the body a good place to start is with what we eat. The SAD diet that most Americans consume is undoubtedly contributing to the decrease in diversity of our body machines internal rainforest.

The Standard American Diet that is full of processed food is sterile and hyper-hygienic, meaning it's free from bacteria and other living organisms. Processed SAD foods contain artificial and unnatural ingredients that could contribute to a break down in the cellular lining of our gut which increases what is known as "gut permeability" which has been shown to increase our risk for developing autoimmune disease and inflammation.[61] Not to mention most SAD food is completely void of fiber that literally feed our gut bacteria and contribute to a thriving inner community. Fiber, which at face value seems like one nutrient, is in a class of hundreds of different fiber structures known as polysaccharides, or complex carbohydrates, from plants that feed various strains of bacteria. Different bugs like different types of fibers so just taking a fiber supplement, which often consist of only one polysaccharide, without eating a variety of plants foods is totally missing the mark.

As I mentioned in the last chapter, you cannot supplement your way out of a diet depleted of SOUL food. We have evolved as a species by consuming the foods that our environment and mama earth has made available to us over thousands of years, so it's naive to assume that by isolating nutrients in human designer combinations or by "creating" our own foods, that we are going to be able to trump nature's woven in wisdom. Without doubt, a diet that is low in fiber from an assortment of SOUL-foods starves our healthy gut bacteria that make up the front lines of our internal defense system.

At this point, you might be a bit overwhelmed with all of the information that you have just read regarding the impact that the gut microbiome has on our health and Body Wisdom. A decrease in sterile, processed SAD foods and in increase in fiber and nutrient-rich SOUL foods needs to occur in order to cultivate a healthy colony of gut bacteria.

The last chapter has had the sole purpose of helping you to understand exactly how important taking care of your gut microbiome is for maintaining good health and preventing dis-ease. It is also meant to reinforce the importance of eating real SOUL food. I want you to know that these changes are possible, and that at a point in my past I was at the same crossroads that you might be at right now. As I've shared, by changing the foods I've consumed over the last 7 or so years, every facet of my life has transformed and taken new shape.

Our Second Brain

When I was in my early twenties and transitioning into eating plant-based, I didn't have all the information I have now. While I am still constantly learning as new science is released to the public, the benefits of consuming foods that feed the trillions of creatures living inside me has been far reaching. When I began my journey, I was too naive to second guess my doctor's prescription of medications to combat depression and anxiety. My later newfound awareness of how pharmaceuticals impact my inner ecosystem proved that some of my intuition on how to heal my body naturally was accurate. My physical, emotional and mental hiccups with foods were all dramatically improved by changing the foods I ate and I now know it was in part due to changes in my gut bacteria.

By shifting my focus from weight-loss and to focusing on my health (and that of the planet) made the transition a more empowering experience. Upping my intake of SOUL foods including starchy vegetables, and soluble and insoluble fiber-rich plants began to shift and cultivate new life that had a direct impact on who I was as a person. One of the reasons our gut is called "the second brain" is because the neurons that line the walls of our intestines have a lot to say to our main brain upstairs. When we upset this balance and starve off beneficial bacteria by consuming SAD foods, the ability of our gut to produce neurotransmitters that stabilize our mood and make us happy is inhibited. Most of the manufacturing of these feel good chemicals lies within the walls of our bellies. Although they get released in the brain and body when we hug, kiss, smile, or think of something positive their creation is directly related to our microscopic friends and the food we choose to eat.

As we've touched on before, it's a new idea to look to the gut to balance out mood disorders like anxiety and depression which ultimately affect how we eat. With the little bit of information that we do have, it make sense that someone who lacks motivation, drive, excitement or passion in their life might just need to tend to their inner bacterial wilderness. As I mentioned earlier, there are predominant neurotransmitters that are produced in the gut that heavily influence how we show up in the world. [62] Dopamine is the neurotransmitter associated with motivation. Be it motivation to start new tasks, finish old ones, or to exercise. Research suggests that the best way to increase dopamine levels is to work out, but you have to have the initial motivation to move your body in the first place. A good place to start is by promoting the growth of the good guys in the gut.

Struggling to find the motivation to break a sweat could induce feelings of failure and be tangled up with sunken levels of serotonin, the neurotransmitter linked with mood and excitement. Low serotonin means few things will bring you joy or perhaps that which used to make you happy no longer elicits the same response. Forget having a favorite food, song, movie or activity. People who are sort of laissez faire to everything might not be truly depressed, they could very well have subpar neurotransmitter production due to poor gut health. Even our body's ability to respond to stress is influenced by the guts ability to produce GABA, a "calm down" neurotransmitter tasked with the responsibility to regulate anxiety by being an inhibitory neurotransmitter. When our bodies production of these good mood chemicals dwindles, our inner light dims. Have you ever heard yourself say "I just don't feel like myself?" Well here is some insight into why and it could have to do with the food you eat and bacterial community inside you.

We might be struggling to make sound decisions, calm our nerves or respond to stress in a way that doesn't result in the questioning of our sanity. We may no longer be interested in things that were once our favorites. While it's easy to just assume that something is wrong with us, it might behoove us all to accept that the ecosystem inside the walls of our intestines works both independently but also in conjunction with our brain to influence our actions.

Upon learning about this connection, it's easy to understand why the food we eat is in so many ways one of the most influential elements in our lives. With the revelatory understanding of the role our gut bacteria plays in our personality, the whole idea of "trusting your gut" is actually well rooted in science and not just a cliché word phrase. The pit of our stomach has ancient microbes living within that are always responding to our physical environment and surroundings, which means you very well might "know in your gut something to be true."

An integral part of Body Wisdom is healing the gut and then learning to listen to it. The road to healing starts at the grocery store and then with every meal and each individual bite of food. It doesn't take much to nurture your gut, and the components of a gut-friendly diet are already at supermarket and farmers markets. The less processed a food the more beneficial it likely is. Keep in mind that the gut needs both prebiotic and probiotic foods. Prebiotic foods are high in a special type of fiber that feed the gut bugs and support digestive health, while probiotics are healthy strains of bacteria that support the growth of healthy bacteria in your gut to help break down and ferment food.

To get you started on your gut bacteria make-over below are some suggestions of foods to incorporate!

Prebiotic foods that I love:
Asparagus, onions, garlic, banana, sweet potatoes, wheat bran, chicory root, dandelion greens, barley, oats, apples, flaxseed, jicama, seaweed.

Probiotic foods that I love:
Sauerkraut, kimchi, pickles, yogurt such as unsweetened coconut yogurt that you make (I love the Minimalistbaker.com recipe), and other fermented foods.

To give you a page from my daily gut protocol playbook, one of the easiest ways for me to make sure I take care of my gut is to get in a lot of leafy green vegetables which are high in a sulfur-based sugar and fiber that feed the gut bacteria. I also like to chomp down a generous spoonful of sauerkraut most days. Taking care of the wild internal system of your body machine doesn't need to be complicated or interfere with your routine. An extra minute a day is all you need to eat a big spoonful of sauerkraut and just be sure to grab leafy greens with every trip to the market to eat with every meal.

Again this does not have to complicated or overwhelming. It can be easy, stress-free and dare I say fun.

Chapter 6 ACTION STEPS:

Discovery #1: For the next week give your gut a makeover. On the first day of this week write down how you are feeling including notes about your energy, presence of bloat, inflammation, digestion, skin, mental clarity, mood, motivation and sleep quality.

Discovery #2: Next, include SOUL food at every meal. Add leafy greens to every meal, it can be as little as ½ cup to a massive kale salad. Just get 'em in with every meal if you can, and eat a bite of sauerkraut each day. On day seven write down how you are feeling and then compare.

7

GETTING TO THE SOURCE
DIGESTIVE DIS-EASE
AND ELIMINATION DIETS

"Remember, you don't eliminate your reset foods because they were bad or unhealthy, you eliminated them to see how they worked for you."

—Melissa Hartwig

N ow that you understand the importance of eating a diet that is full of SOUL food and only sometimes eating processed, packaged, food-like products for gut health and overall wellbeing, let's dive deeper into another huge component going on in our gut that is involved in helping your beautiful body machine run at full capacity. Anytime you eat a meal, your body goes through a series of steps that help you to absorb and utilize all of the nutrition from your food. The primary mechanisms involved in the digestion and assimilation of nutrients take action in our digestive system. When we talk about the quality or efficiency of our digestive ability, what we are really talking about is the robustness of our gut health. As you just learned, the gut refers to not only the physical organs involved in digestion such as the stomach, small intestine, and large intestine (colon), but also a fascinating colony of friendly bacterial organisms known as your gut microbiome.

Since our gut houses 70% of our immune system, our overall health is intricately connected to the health of our gut.[63] Our digestive system is in many ways our first line of defense against sickness and is also heavily involved in preventing the progression of disease. Having a gut that excels in the process of digesting food and absorbing nutrients is the foundational component involved in the operational capacity of our body. It is through the process of digestion that our body absorbs the precious nutrients from our food that it needs to thrive so that it can create health and vibrancy from the inside out. There are a variety of digestive upsets that can interrupt this process, and these can make the act of nourishing our bodies challenging and sometimes painful.

Digestive *Dis-ease*

Digestive *dis-ease* can lead to negative symptoms of an upset GI tract and can be caused by a number of different issues ranging from Irritable Bowel Syndrome (IBS), constipation, diarrhea, bloating and gas. These are challenging on their own to deal with, but when left untreated can lead to systemic issues such as asthma, exhaustion, food allergies and even chronic health issues. While the foods we eat are the starting lineup in the game of well-being, digestion is the star quarterback of our internal health team.

Digestion works to break down, absorb, and integrate the nutrients contained in the foods we ingest. All of the cells in our body that make up our hair, skin, and tissues get their fuel from the food, water and air we take in from the outside world. If our system is not running optimally, then organs (like our liver and pancreas) have to work in overtime, which impacts the amount of nourishment our body receives from the foods we eat. When dealing with any type of digestive discomfort the first step to take is to look at the food we are eating.

Everybody is uniquely different, so one-size fits all fad diets and food trends from the outside world are not the best place to turn when looking for answers with digestive issues. By blocking out the opinions of others we can give a closer listen to what our body tells us and build up a solid knowledge foundation of what works and what doesn't. This means you will have to spend more time tuning inward and paying attention to how you feel after every meal, especially when eating certain foods that you suspect are problematic.

This often means slowing down in this fast-paced world of ours and taking time to enjoy your meal. As difficult as it may sound to pause and take inventory of how we feel when we eat, this is a critical step in developing Body Wisdom that will set you up to take control of your health and empower you to choose how you want to feel each day. This also means paying attention to your mood and stress level as well because it can inhibit your body's ability to digest your food properly contributing to the issues. This is something for you to keep in mind because while the food is very important, how we are thinking about food and our bodies plays a huge role, which we will further discuss later in the book. For now though, we will continue to talk about the food.

Why Bio-Individuality Is So Important

Just because one person can eat a certain food and feel fine doesn't mean it will be the same for you. As we briefly discussed earlier, common foods that causes digestive upset or allergies are corn, eggs, wheat/gluten/grains, soy, dairy, peanuts and tree nuts, fish, shellfish, sweeteners, preservatives, artificial ingredients, or a class of vegetables called nightshades including ashwagandha, eggplant, peppers, tomatoes, and potatoes. Some people are even sensitive to onions and garlic. One or several of these ingredients could potentially be a culprit for any number of things you might be experiencing.

The key to feeling vibrant is in identifying what foods agree with you. There are a number of tools available to help you determine what's best, and these range from expensive lab tests or at home kits to elimination diets or a good old fashioned food journal. Regardless of the method you choose, having awareness of triggering foods can be a powerful tool. Even mild symptoms like bloating are worth paying attention to as they are an indication of what is happening internally and pieces of information from your body.

Fabulous Fiber

In addition to uncovering food intolerance or allergies, another step to improve your digestive well-being and gut health is to incorporate more fiber into your diet. Most dietary recommendations state that women should get 25-35g of fiber while men should get 35-45 g of fiber as a minimum each day. Have you ever paid attention to how much fiber you eat in a day? Typically, I am not for counting anything when it comes to our food, but if you truly have no idea how much fiber you are getting it might be a good idea to take a look to determine if increasing your fiber could be helpful. You can do this by increasing your vegetable intake or evaluating where your diet stacks up to this recommendation by looking at the fiber content of the foods your typically eat. If you are like most Americans, you probably need more fiber in your diet. With that being said, simply adding in more fiber too quickly to a fiber depleted diet can induce bloating, gas, and discomfort. So if you need to bump up your consumption of fabulous fiber, do so slowly over the course of a month or two. Don't just dive face first into fiber rich foods, as you will likely experience some intense stomach discomfort. Slow and steady is the name of the game.

Feed Your Family of Gut Bugs

As you just learned, fiber does not only help balance our blood sugar, but it is also literal food for our gut microbiome! When we eat foods that contain fiber, the friendly gut bugs in our large intestine break down the fiber in a process known as fermentation. If we introduce too much fiber too quickly, our gut bugs throw themselves a little fermentation party and this can produce excess gas, bloat, and pain. That does not necessarily mean that you should avoid fiber-rich foods, rather start to incorporate moderate amounts slowly over a long period of time to allow your digestive system to adapt and adjust.

Foods like beans, lentils, raw and cooked veggies including cabbage or cauliflower can initially upset our stomach. This is due to the excess fermentation of these fibers similar to how eating too fast or drinking carbonated beverages can cause your stomach to get in a pinch. But this initial upset is not the case for every person. Each of us has a unique ecosystem inside with variations from our genetics, upbringing, the environment and lifestyle, mood and stress level, which means we all need to eat a bit differently to best fuel our unique body system. These factors will play a role in how that internal system operates and what types of fuel it needs to thrive.

This is why it is so important to pay attention to how you feel after you eat certain things. My best friend gets nauseous after eating avocados, and as you probably know if you follow me on instagram (@caraskitchen), I feel like I can conquer the world after eating an avocado. If we always listen to the outside world about what is healthy and good for us, then how are we supposed to discover what our insanely wise body is saying?

Tune In to Tune Out Digestive *Dis-ease*

To jumpstart the discovery process, the following table contains a list of whole foods and food derivatives that have been known to contribute to autoimmune diseases, digestive disorders, bloating, brain fog and chronic illness. This is not an absolute complete list, but it will help steer you in the right direction in determining what potential foods are triggering discomfort.

Corn	Nightshades	Grains	Dairy	Soy	Nuts	Other
Citric acid	Ashwagandha	Wheat	Whey	Carob	Cashew	Alcohol
Confection sugar	Potatoes	Rice	Casein	Emulsifiers	Almond	Shellfish
fructose	Eggplant	Quinoa	Lactose	Guar gum	Walnut	Eggs
Dextrin Dextrose lactic acid Malt monoso-dium	Hot peppers including jalapeno, red pepper, cayenne	Enriched flour	Cheese	Natural flavors, Shoyu, Miso	Peanuts	Processed food
Mono- and Diglycerides	Paprika	Barley,	Yogurt	Soy lecithin	Peas	Sugar
Glutamate	Goji berries	Bran	Ice cream	Vegetable gum	Beans	Fast food
Sorbitol	Tomatoes	Oats		Tempeh	Lentils	
Starch				Textured vegetable protein		

Table 2 [64] Food allergies can be a life-threatening immune response to a particular food, whereas a food intolerance or a sensitivity is a less severe immune response. Think of it this way, food allergies produce a huge immune response where a ton of antibodies are recruited to attack the offending food, but sensitivities and intolerances produce a low-grade immune response that causes inflammation but is not necessarily life-threatening in an immediate sense. In essence, a food sensitivity means that you might feel discomfort but it is not life threatening.

When the Immune System Malfunctions

Our immune system is not designed to attack the foods we eat, however sometimes it makes errors and creates antibodies to the unique proteins found in our food. It is possible that our immune system can stop producing certain antibodies to offending foods, but it can take time, and will require the complete elimination of the reactive food. It is believed that once created, antibodies can clear the system, but it may take anywhere from three to six weeks, sometimes longer for this process to take place. If you believe you are someone who has developed a food sensitivity, or intolerance, there are lab tests available that test for antibodies. This is a valuable test to have done if you suspect you are reacting to certain foods, but be aware of the price as these tests can cost upwards of $600. If these test are not available within your budget, there is a much more affordable way to determine food sensitivities and that is through the use of an elimination diet.

Elimination Diets

An Elimination Diet is a regimented but temporary way of eating that removes certain foods linked to allergies and illness such as digestive issues, brain fog and fatigue. For the sake of this chapter I want to emphasize that when using the term "diet" in regards to an "elimination diet" I am not talking about the same type of dieting that we use culturally to lose weight. I do not want the word, for the sake of this chapter, to be emotionally triggering. You are not good or bad based on the types of foods you eat or if you follow an elimination diet. You can think of it as a protocol or a program that is used for nutrition and Body Wisdom only.

These types of elimination protocols or programs are meant to be a tool in helping you learn about your body and how different foods make it feel. To really narrow down what impacts you, it is sometimes necessary to eliminate the triggering foods for at least 30 days. In theory, this can allow antibodies to clear from your system giving it an opportunity to reset. One way to look at an elimination diet is like a system refresh on a computer. If your computer is running slowly or acting buggy then you might empty the trash bin, remove some unnecessary files from the hard drive to clear up some space, and maybe update the software to then restart the computer.

An elimination diet is like a good clean up of our internal system and hardware. We take out all the unnecessary, possibly harmful foods, clean house, and then restart. Throughout the 30 days, you could start to notice a significant difference in how you are feeling mentally, emotionally and physically. After the 30 days is complete, the goal is to re-incorporate the suspect foods in a systematic fashion so that the problematic food(s) can be identified.

People can be resistant to uncovering the source of their digestive *dis-ease* because they have found a way to manage their symptoms and removing foods that are loved can be challenging. However, there is a huge difference between managing your symptoms and eliminating them all together. For example, if you are reacting to dairy, but continue to consume it with the help of Lactaid, (a common digestive aid for dairy) your body is still producing inflammatory compounds that can cause damage to healthy cells and the immune system which can lead to painful side effects and even chronic disease. However, if you were to eliminate dairy all-together, then you would not only be addressing the root cause of your digestive *dis-ease*, but you would also allow your whole-body inflammation to calm down and potentially help your body to heal and feel better. For years, I ate dairy without knowing it was making me feel so lousy. Because I now care so much about feeling good, I have very little desire to eat it, even though I know I could if I wanted to.

Let's Talk About Triggers

Eating a triggering food not only makes us feel lousy, but it also becomes majorly taxing on our immune system's defense mechanism and healing abilities. We become more susceptible to the common cold and can even begin to age faster. If you're not yet sold on the benefits of an elimination diet/protocol, here are some additional health concerns you could potentially reverse that would allow you to experience the whole-body benefits of eliminating offending foods:

Chronic fatigue

Arthritis

Asthma

Nutrient deficiencies

Mood disorders including anxiety and depression

Skin problems like acne, hives and eczema

Learning disabilities

Difficulty sleeping or insomnia

Autoimmune disorders

Cognitive function and decline

Headaches

Muscle and joint pain like arthritis

Kidney and gallbladder problems

Source:[65] You can absolutely create your own elimination diet (or program/protocol) if you have an idea of what foods you are reacting to. Another option is to follow the guidance of a programmed elimination diet such as Whole30 or The Clean Program.

Popular Elimination Diets: Whole30

Whole30 is a 30-day elimination diet where you remove foods that could potentially have a negative impact on your health. According to their website, the Whole30 is designed to "eliminate the most common craving-inducing, blood sugar disrupting, gut-damaging, inflammatory food groups for a full 30 days."[66] It is designed to allow your body to heal and recover from whatever affects these inflammatory foods may be causing. In line with the computer analogy I presented before, the Whole30 is a way to push the reset button with your health so as to improve the downstream physical and psychological effects of the food choices you've been making. By completing an elimination diet, you will not only learn how the foods you've been eating are affecting your day-to-day life, but you will also strengthen your connection to foods that promote long term health, and overall intuition around food.[67] I don't agree with every aspect of Whole30 because some of the teachings do go against the grain of what I inherently believe and stand for, so please don't interpret my sharing of it or participation in it as a full stamp of approval. Naturally, I like to engage in and experience things for myself before I form an opinion on something. That said, I do like the tough love language Melissa uses. While tough love is not everyone's cup of tea, it sure is my personal shot of whiskey. It's worth noting that I was raised on tough love, so some straightforward honest truth speaking doesn't offend me but I know that is not the case for everyone. Sometimes a more compassionate approach is more effective, it comes down to you personally, so remember to stay true to what feels most right to you.

Melissa really drives home the importance of fully committing to the program for 30 full days and explains that while it is hard, it's not nearly as hard as so many other things in life. Looking at it comparatively, to say raising a child or fighting cancer, eating whole real foods for 30 days is easy and in fact how most humans ate for most of our existence. She says it will change your life, and while I think that might sound a bit far-reaching upon delivery, I do believe it has the potential to create some major shifts in the experience of being in your body.

Another Popular Elimination Diet: The Clean Program

Another popular tool to aid you in an elimination diet/protocol/program is The Clean Program. It is a 21-day elimination diet that includes supplements and shakes. A point of differentiation with

The Clean Program vs the Whole30 is that it is similar in structure to Intermittent Fasting, which means you only eat food within a certain window of time so that you can allow your body the opportunity to fully digest the food you have eaten. The Clean Program advocates that you create a 12-hour window of fasting (for example, from 7pm — 7am) so that your body can activate its natural healing abilities. On their site they say that they "believe you already hold the keys to your health, and we want to help you unlock the door. In just 21 days you can see real transformation, and set healthy habits for life." They provide you with shake mixes for breakfast and dinner as well as supplements and probiotics. The list of foods to include and exclude are slightly different from Whole30 as well. The Clean Program allows non-gluten grains like rice and buckwheat, some legumes like lentils and garbanzo beans, and non-nutritive sweeteners, all of which are not allowed on Whole30. Conversely, some fruits, animal protein, eggs and coffee are off limits on The Clean Program but allowed on Whole30.

What I find interesting is that while the promised outcomes of these two diets/protocols and programs are similar, they provide a different road map to get there. What this reinforces is that there are many different ways to accomplish the same goal, and the path of one person may not be the path of another.

As I've said before everybody is different and you have to *do you.*

Whether you want to start an elimination diet or not, it's important to check in and be really honest with yourself about how efficiently your beautiful body machine is operating. Embarking on a 21-30 day plan to resolve your gut, hormone, or energy issues requires a firm commitment, but also involves a focus on balance. For some people who have struggled in the past with yo-yo dieting, crash diets or binge eating, I recommend being fully present to why you want to do an elimination diet before setting forth to complete one. If you approach an elimination diet with the goal of weight loss or healing your relationship with food, you may be setting yourself up for more stress and upset. However, if you approach an elimination diet with the goal of improving your health and digestive wellbeing, you may find that you gain a whole new appreciation for the healing ability of your body. Your mindset and mental health make all the difference which is why I do not recommend them for everyone.

Checking In With Yourself Before Starting An Elimination Diet

While having food sensitivities and digestive issues on their own are tough to manage and an elimination diet can help, having an unhealthy relationship to food adds another layer of complexity. Let's say for example someone is allergic to wheat and needs to avoid it for health issues. A "normal eater" might choose to still eat wheat and have a response that isn't emotionally negative. They might say "well this looks good, I am going to eat, but might pay for it later and feel sick." End of story. This is very much like my relationship to dairy now.

Where as someone who has a disordered relationship with food might anticipate the physical discomfort and also wrap it up with layers of guilt and shame. You probably regularly tell yourself not to eat something or that you shouldn't eat something. Then you might eat that food, anticipate the physical discomfort and tell yourself that "you are disgusting, horrible person who can't be trusted around food." So if you fall into the latter category, keep in mind that healing our relationship with food, meaning removing the guilt, shame and obsession with body size, needs to be addressed first because it will help you navigate food sensitivities and digestive dis-ease while developing your Body Wisdom.

We will address your relationship with food in depth throughout the remainder of this book but paying attention to the physical sensations after you eat food and prioritizing those signals from your body over the internal monologue or external dialogue is key in this process.

It's important to be in a mentally and emotionally stable place not only with your relationship to yourself, but also with food so you don't backfire and end up binge eating. While elimination diets can be a phenomenal tool for someone with underlying health issues, I would not recommended it for anyone with an eating disorder, whose main goal is weight loss or who is stuck in a *diet mentality*.

For the purpose of clarity when using the term "diet" in the *diet mentality*, I am referring to a certain way of eating that we become emotionally attached to because we see ourselves as either good or bad for eating a certain way. Or we believe that there is a right or wrong way to eat. Often this means "dieting" is a way of achieving a desired physical appearance. A *diet mentality* is a mental framework where we trap ourselves in a cycle of only eating enough OR only eating certain foods in order to control the way our bodies look. A *diet mentality* is always wrapped up in control and some form of morality.

Diets from this perspective are often viewed as short-term because we don't intend to eat in the prescribed way for very long. This is one of the reasons why diets are so appealing to so many people. *Eat this way for 30 days and get the body of your dreams and heal your relationship with food.* It's a really seductive promise. So before you consider embarking on a 21-30 elimination diet, consider how you interpret the purpose of this plan. Is it to improve your skin, gut health, energy levels, and hormone balance? Or is to lose weight quickly, heal your relationship with food and achieve a specific physical appearance? Is it to control yourself around food because you are often so out of control? If you find yourself in the camp of the latter, or even with the majority of your reason being on weight-loss, structure and control, I encourage you to consider if you are living your life from a *diet mentality* which is inhibiting your ability to develop Body Wisdom.

When we find ourselves at the point where we are tired and fed-up with our body's appearance, we often feel that a "diet" will be a quick fix to help us be more happy with ourselves. Which often means we think that restricting food is the answer. Whether our desire to go on a diet is based on legitimate health concerns or dissatisfaction with our physical appearance or relationship with food, we end up going on them for the structure and promise of body satisfaction they provide. Typically we are not happy with the way that we look so we want to make a change in how we eat in order to look a certain way.

However, if we approach these changes from a *"diet mentality"*, we are more likely to heavily restrict calories or remove entire food groups as a way to manipulate our body size. What I hear so many of my clients tell me is that they were ok with the structure in place but then resorted back to old patterns and ways of being once the structure was eliminated. This is almost always because of the mindset we had entering into the diet/program/protocol. We have to change how we think about food not just change the food we eat and following a prescribe way of eating or diet does not address the mandatory element of our mindset.

And even when we do our best to follow the diet plan to a T, approaching change from this perspective often results in minor slip-ups feeling like a massive failure, and this shame and guilt can lead to binge eating (again the mindset pieces). After we binge, we tell ourselves that we messed up today, so the entire day is a wash and I should just eat everything in sight because the "diet starts again tomorrow." Sound familiar? This mindset can create or perpetuate an unhealthy relationship with food. Its why so many of us are stuck in a diet-binge cycle with very little balance.

Ditch the Damn Wagon

It's truly hard to "fall off the wagon" when there is no wagon. In order to break free from this mindset and vicious cycle of dieting, binging and restricting, we have to mentally remove the wagon. This is the type of mindset shift that would need to occur before I would recommend an elimination diet (program/protocol), otherwise it might not actually make a difference for you. Elimination diets are not an intuitive eating process as your food options are limited for a very specific purpose. Elimination diets are meant to be looked at as a tool for understanding your Body Wisdom and discovering what foods work best for you. Using the information gained to intuitively eat can be a very valuable experience, but if used improperly can become a tool for self-degradation and lead to a more disordered relationship with food.

I encourage you to really be honest with yourself and consider your mental framework when you think about an elimination diet. If the idea of eliminating foods like dairy, gluten, soy, and sugar puts you in a deprivation mindset, I suggest that you pause and instead redirect your focus on developing your Body Wisdom through the practice of *Intuitive Eating* which I discuss in the next chapter.

Chapter 7 ACTION STEPS:

Discovery #1: Intuitively, what foods causes digestive upset for you? Does the idea of not eating these foods feel restrictive and limiting? Do you like the structure and rules, and see it as a diet to lose weight? Or does the idea of not eating these foods because you truly care about feeling good inspire you to honor your body?

Discovery #2: When you think about an elimination diet (aka program or protocol) what thoughts come up for you? What types of outcomes do you think it will provide? How much does the idea of potential weight loss influence your desire to complete or not complete and elimination diet/program/protocol?

8
INTUITIVE EATING FOR BODY WISDOM

"Intuitive eaters march to their inner hunger signals, and eat whatever they choose without experiencing guilt or an ethical dilemma."

—Evelyn Tribole

E ating intuitively in order to discover what makes you feel best might sound like some crazy new age shit, but it's actually quite the opposite. Fundamentally, Intuitive Eating refers to the ability to eat regular, nourishing meals and foods that you truly love from a rational perspective as opposed to a perspective of food attachment, morality, guilt, shame, deprivation, or restriction. It's about paying attention to how food affects you physically and mentally. Intuitive eating is a practice of eating when you are hungry and stopping when you are full but also allowing yourself to eat for the sake of pleasure and enjoyment which means you might not always be hungry. It is not a diet, but rather a practice of bringing awareness to yourself mentally, emotionally and physically before, during and after the eating process.

The purpose of approaching food this way is to disassociate from a diet-based way of thinking and instead approach food from the perspective of nourishment and satisfaction. As children, we were the original intuitive eaters before the outside world started to influence or try to control our food intake.

To help you understand the distinction let's explore the difference in mindset of a dieter vs. an intuitive eater. The stream of consciousness from a dieter who is considering having a piece of bread might go along the lines of this:

"How many calories or carbs does it have?"

"What do I have to not eat later to make up for it?"

"If I eat this bread then I've ruined my diet so I might as well eat all those cookies over there too."

"Oh well, I can restart my diet tomorrow."

This mentality of analyzing food and being very emotionally attached to the way we eat interferes with our ability to make the connection between what we eat and how we feel from a physical standpoint. It also interrupts our ability to gain pleasure and satisfaction from food.

When our mindset is in the realm of a dieter, we often have shame and guilt wrapped up in our food choices if they do not look a certain way and this inhibits our ability to develop Body Wisdom. We have to slowly untangle the knot between the food choices we make and the disordered thoughts in our mind. We start this process by creating awareness around our emotional triggers so that we can begin to understand how we are using food. The wise and sassy Isabel Foxen Duke, a fellow health coach, explains the three main reasons why people eat. As you read about them below, see which way resonates with you most.

Biologically Imperative

The first reason to eat is for physical nourishment and the alleviation of physical hunger. This refers to the most primal reason to eat food in that we sense hunger through physical sensation, and respond by choosing to nourish our body. People who eat for this reason are often emotionally unattached to food because from this perspective, food is simply biologically essential for survival. It is solely about physical and biological nourishment of our body and life sustaining.

Emotional Eating

The second reason to eat is for emotional nourishment or fulfillment. People who eat in this fashion typically find that they search for food in response to boredom, depression, anger, sadness or stress. As humans we all need coping mechanisms from time to time. While some emotional eating can be potentially unhealthy because it can numb us to the underlying cause of our unmet emotional needs, not all emotional eating is bad or something that needs to be avoided.

Having cake at a wedding or on your birthday is a perfectly healthy form of emotional eating. There is no biological nourishment from birthday cake, but the emotional satisfaction of enjoying food in celebration with our friends and family is an important aspect of what it represents to our culture. Food can be communal or spiritual in nature, so it's important to understand that having some wine to celebrate a promotion at work or a piece of chocolate to reward yourself for accomplishing a goal is a perfectly acceptable reason to eat, even if it is purely driven by emotions. It's also A-OK to get some ice cream after a break up to comfort yourself, you're a human being with loads of emotions and we are hardwired to receive pleasure from food.

The same goes for having something cozy like hot chocolate if you are feeling a little down. It's ok to use food as a coping mechanism sometimes, but it does turn problematic when it becomes our primary coping mechanism, or if we guilt and shame ourselves for eating emotionally. At the same time, restricting ourselves of food in times of celebration or sadness creates a mindset of deprivation, which we want to avoid in order to prevent yo-yo dieting and rebound binge eating.

Binge Eating

When emotional eating becomes something we are very ashamed of it often turns into binge eating, or what Isabel referrers to as "shame eating". It can be a response to real deprivation or imagined deprivation and it is always wrapped up in guilt and shame. These feelings are often the distinguishing factor between emotional eating and binge eating. Binge eating is typically the result of depriving ourselves from the foods we want (dieting) or not eating enough food (i.e calorie restriction) which is real deprivation. It can also be the response to not allowing ourselves to actually enjoy food even if we choose to eat it, which is called "imagined deprivation." Binge eating can also be a response driven way of eating because there is perceived deprivation in the future i.e. "diet starts again tomorrow, better eat it all right now." Lastly, binge eating is characterized by consuming food really fast, often in private so no one else can witness the behavior.

Because there is so much body dissatisfaction wrapped up in binge eating, just one bite of an "off-limits food" will likely result in a loss of control and the overconsumption of the restricted foods. Binge eating can also inhibit our ability to enjoy food because we become so concerned that the ice cream, cake, pizza or whatever we are consuming will make us fat.

This mindset and fatphobia often leads us to become obsessive about the food we eat, and this can lead us to overeat because we make ourselves busy obsessing about calories when we could be obsessing about how delicious our food is. Sadly, the guilt and shame are two emotions that do nothing but perpetuate the cycle and instill a lack of self-worth that is rooted in our body image and "lack of control."

When we have low self-esteem or dislike our body, we become very attached to the food we eat because there is a direct link between eating food and how we look. If every time you take a bite of food you are concerned with the impact on your thighs, it's unlikely that you will have a strong sense of power or freedom around food. To become less attached to what we eat, we have to shift the context for food, which is where the principles of intuitive eating come into play.

Intuitive Eating

In the book Intuitive Eating, Evelyn Tribole and Elyse Resch, lay out specific principles to help us rediscover intuitive eating which I briefly discuss throughout the remainder of this chapter. As I mentioned, as children we were natural intuitive eaters because we asked for food when we were hungry, had no moral dilemma when choosing food, and stopped eating when we were full. We were not born with body dissatisfaction, so eating had nothing to do with our body size until someone taught us that.

As we begin to grow up and become socialized, things often begin to shift due to our different life experiences and upbringing. Influence from the outside world all lead us to change the way we feed ourselves, and obsess over the way we look. How many of us remember being told to finish our food by our parents even if we were no longer hungry? As innocent as it may seem, being told to eat more when you are already full starts to throw off our ability to listen to our bodies signals and can lead to developing the habit of eating past the point of being comfortably full or feeling guilty if you leave food on your plate.

Ditch Dieting and Diet Mentality

To get back to our roots we have to ditch the *diet-mentality*, let go of our fear of weight gain all together and learn to connect to our body signals. We have to throw out the "get thin quick schemes" and be prepared to reject new ones if and when they come our way.

We have to open ourselves to viewing food as something other than a function of gaining or losing weight. Instead, we want to start to see food as nourishment, fuel, celebration, cultural expression, and a healing tool. This will allow us to start to honor the hunger and fullness signals from our body and gradually we will begin to trust our ability to eat in a balanced way.

To bring ourselves back into balance and leave behind the impulse to control our eating, we have to stop depriving ourselves of all foods and allow ourselves to eat what we want. It's only when we tell ourselves we can't have something that we find ourselves experiencing an intense drive to eat in "last supper sized portions." This impulse to overeat as a result of food restriction can lead to an overwhelming sense of guilt and shame, which does nothing but degrade our Body Wisdom and make us feel incapable of having a positive relationship with food.

This isn't to say that removing your food rules and giving yourself unconditional permission to eat won't result in a period of eating *all the things*. It is possible that you enter into a rebound phase which is completely normal for some people, but not certain for everyone. If this happens, are you willing to trust the process? Are you willing to not be seduced back into dieting or restricting again, rather move through this temporary period of being a kid in a candy store so to speak until your body starts to balance out? You might feel the urge to go back to your old ways but then you are right back at the beginning of the diet-binge cycle. If you are truly ready to become an intuitive eater you have to be willing for things to be messy and for things to take time. You also have to be willing to remove judgement on yourself and replace it with compassion.

Food Pleasure, Satisfaction and Enjoyment

We have to challenge all the internal chatter about what we can and cannot eat too. It might never go away entirely but we can't allow ourselves to believe that we are "good" or "bad" for what we choose to eat. When was the last time you went out to eat and just ordered whatever you were in the mood for, be it nachos or a kale salad, and didn't attach further meaning on to it? The nachos were not "bad" and they did not mean that you ruined your diet, or that you have to make up for it later. And the kale salad did not mean you were "good" or whatever. It just means that you ordered the food you wanted so you could:

1. Satisfy your hunger, nourish your body and,
2. Gain pleasure and enjoyment from the food.

If you don't really remember the last time then let this act as an alarm bell that you likely have way to many food rules and are stuck operating from a *diet-mentality*. The next time you go out to eat order whatever you want. When we quiet the mind of judgement, we can pay more attention to the body sensations and signals during the eating process. We can pause and ask ourselves:

"Do I really want to eat this?"
"How does this taste?"
"Am I enjoying it?"
"How do I feel?"
"Am I full yet?"

By actually slowing down enough to taste what we are eating, we give ourselves the opportunity to enjoy our food more and this actually leads us to eat less than if we had inhaled our meal. By eating what it is we truly want, we give ourselves permission to feel pleasure from food and this leads to more satisfaction and content. Binge eating or overeating is often the result of not allowing ourselves to enjoy what we are eating while eating it, which is the same thing as depriving ourselves of the food all together. We have to let ourselves receive pleasure from food. You can't just let them eat cake, you have to also enjoy eating the cake.

This also means ordering the nachos if you truly want them instead of ordering the salad because you think you "should." It's unlikely that you will get the same satisfaction from the salad if you truly wanted nachos, which could lead to binge eating.

Honor our Emotions

Once we have decided that we are going to work on becoming on intuitive eater and develop the ability to let ourselves enjoy food, we can begin to explore other ways to honor our emotions without the sole use of food. While eating is partly emotional in and of itself, meaning we get pleasure from it, like sex or engaging in an activity that we love, we want to address the root causes of our emotions. Experiencing sadness, loneliness, anxiety, boredom, and fear are all normal parts of life and while food might offer temporary reprieve, it will not solve the underlying issues of why these sometimes painful emotions are present.

Uncovering alternative ways to honor your emotions is fundamental to changing your relationship with food. In the long run, a donut will not make you less lonely, a burger will not make you less sad, and a cookie will not make you less anxious. In short, food might offer short-term effectiveness at alleviating these emotions but it is highly unlikely that this will provide long-term effectiveness.

Being a human can be rough, but part of the human experience is learning to love all parts of who you are, even the painful aspects we would rather avoid and mask with food. If you are using food as a coping mechanism, then that is a good indication that there is something else going on in your life that needs to be addressed. While having my eating disorder was very painful, I know that it helped me get through very challenging times because I would turn to it to soothe my emotional duress from other areas of my life. Eventually though, the ED became way more painful to live with so I had to address the sources of my emotional duress head on.

Body Acceptance

In addition to addressing the external and internal sources of emotional duress, a key part of honoring all aspects of your humanity is to accept and love your body exactly as it is. Realizing that there is not just one right way to look even though the media, medical system and diet culture has lead us to believe otherwise. So much of our obsessiveness around food can be the result of trying to manipulate the way our bodies look to fit into this ideal. It is when our self-worth is wrapped up in our size that we become epically emotional around food and use it as our primary coping mechanism.

In order to free our grip on what we eat, we have to accept and love the skin we are in. There is no alternative route. As long as we hate our bodies or ourselves, we will be controlled by food, and we will view our bodies as a prison rather than a vehicle to experience more of what life has to offer. As Martin Luther King Jr. famously said "darkness cannot drive out darkness; only light can do that. Hate cannot drive out hate; only love can do that." We have to accept, appreciate and learn to love our body machines as they are and then we will be able to view food as a way to serve our body, rather than punish it.

Many women (and men too) have a lot of objections to body acceptance or unconditionally loving their body as it is right now, regardless of whether or not they want to make changes. Too often we make our love for ourselves conditional on how we measure up to the outside world's beauty standards which, seeing as almost all images are digitally manipulated, is damn near impossible to achieve.

Some objections include:

"I can't love myself at this size"

"If I accept my body I will stay fat or get more fat"

"No one else can love me at this size"

"What about my health"

These are very limiting beliefs to have about body acceptance. No matter what size you are, you can choose to accept your body and not let it keep you from living the life you want. And working on self-love will absolutely empower you to take action in alignment with your health and wellbeing. Additionally, giving yourself love does not mean you can't continue to make behavioral and lifestyle changes that honor your Body Wisdom, it simply means you are getting on your own team. Here are some steps to do this.

First, the belief that no one else can love you as you are, or the judgement you receive from others, is most likely at the root of this since we only learned to not love our bodies from others first. The outside world taught us that we are not as valuable as someone in a smaller body. That is not something we would ever actually make up ourselves because it is disempowering to anyone who does not fit the arbitrary body size we are told we are supposed to have.

We would never make up the story that cellulite is gross, stretch marks are ugly and anything but a size two (2) is too big. Why the fuck would we make that up? We wouldn't. Rather this belief is something we have learned from our external world, that we have consequently internalized and made our own truth. By believing this we are basically complicit in the oppression that we face as women, so instead of fighting your fat, why don't we fight the fatphobia, weight stigma and judgement of others based on body size? That is a fight worth your time, not the time you invest in fighting against yourself.

Second, our belief about our worth based on our body size absolutely influences how we interact with others which will of course influence how they perceive and interact with us. If you view yourself as beautiful and worthy of respect and acceptance, you are far more likely to receive respect and acceptance than if you believe otherwise.

Third, and the last common objection, what about your health, is a huge can of worms. In short, your weight is a very poor indication of your health. Especially since health is so much more than your physical body size and incorporates your thoughts, stress, relationships, fulfillment in life and your physical well-being which has nothing to do with size at all. There are plenty of people of all shapes and sizes who are fit and healthy just like there are people of all shapes and sizes with chronic disease and illness.

Even though I just addressed some of the most common objections, body acceptance might be very challenging for you to even consider right now, but we have to let go of trying to manipulate our body size in order to heal our relationship with food and develop our Body Wisdom. This is another important reason to tune out the outside world when it comes to how we see ourselves and how we eat. It completely interrupts our ability to hear what our body is saying.

These endless messages that try to convince us that we "aren't good enough" do nothing but attempt to manipulate us into trying the new trendy diets or products so that we can lose weight and fit into the strict parameters of what it means to be "beautiful and healthy" in our culture. Given the bountiful barrage of perfectly toned models used to sell everything from cheeseburgers to cat food, it's no wonder so many women struggle with body image and their relationship with food. If we think in the framework of Body Wisdom where we are striving to create vibrancy in our body, it is obvious that societal pressures and its effect on body image only make a healthy relationship with food harder to achieve.

The stereotype that health isn't available at every size creates a stigma (or shame) around weight that continues to degrade our sense of self-worth. With our weakened esteem, we might find that it is easier to turn over our power to food, because at least we can derive some comfort from the act of eating. I often hear my clients tell me that they numb or check out while binge eating, like they are on auto pilot as if it allows them to momentarily not be present to how they feel about themselves and their life.

However, when we let food control our emotions, we may find that how we eat takes on the ability to dictate how confident we feel. For example, if we are not feeling body positive we might skip a night out with our friends to stay in with Ben and Jerry's ice cream, which then perpetuates the cycle of shame and guilt. Weight stigmas, body shaming, and beauty standards not only affect our relationship with food, but it also impacts our confidence at work, in relationships, and how we relate to exercise.

Intuitive Movement

If we approach the issue of weight stigma, body shaming, and impossible beauty standards from the perspective of wanting to love our bodies, the goal shifts from trying to "fit the mold" to just wanting to feel GOOD. Wanting to feel good doesn't just start and stop with food, it involves your mental health, spiritual health, and of course your physical health. Our bodies were designed to move and be in motion. When this process is interrupted due to a hectic work schedule, lack of motivation, or even shame around your body's appearance, we often find that our lives are lacking in a sense of true fulfillment that we all crave. The way in which we choose to move our bodies through different types of exercise and active living are very influential in how we feel about ourselves from a physical and mental perspective. Exercise, or movement in general, does wonders for increasing your sense of calm, joy, and grounded-ness.

If we approach exercise from the mentality that our bodies need to be punished with exercise because of something we ate or how they look, we can easily find ourselves engaging in militant exercise routines that are not about taking care of ourselves. This approach makes exercise something we "hate to" or "should be" doing instead of something we want to do because it is fun and feels good. It doesn't ever feel good to approach exercise from a place of shameful obligation because we don't like the way we look.

An important component of Body Wisdom is developing a sacred balance between physical nourishment and physical movement. We have to shift our relationship with exercise away from being a penalty for enjoying a piece of cake or to solely lose weight. Exercise can be an enjoyable aspect of your lifestyle, but it needs to become a form of celebration for what our body can do in order for this shift to occur. In essence we want to come from a place of authentic inspiration to take care of ourselves and our bodies. When trying to figure out what to do, start with what you love. What types of exercise do you actually enjoy doing? That's what matters most. Not the amount of calories you burn, or what's best to tone your muscles and give you a tight ass.

Movement impacts our health in far greater ways than just external appearances. The benefits of exercise are far reaching, and include a positive impact on our motivation, stress levels, energy, ability to sleep, focus, our mood, ability to sense hunger and satiety signals and sense of wellbeing. When we want to work out solely for the purpose of losing weight, we will discover that finding motivation can be difficult and it literally sucks the fun and joy right out of it.

However, when we exercise because it makes us feel good and improves our quality of life, it's much easier to commit. Once we find an activity we enjoy, we will look forward to our workouts as opposed to dread them. This creates a beautiful cycle where you naturally want to move, but also encourages us to honor our body with nourishing food after exercise as an act of gratitude for all it can do. In essence, when we do things that feel good but also honor our body, we feel encouraged to continue this cycle of positive action, and by continuing this cycle is how you transform your health and your relationship to food and develop Body Wisdom.

Although the topic of honoring your body through physical movement could fill the pages of its own book, the purpose of this section was to address how we can use exercise in very unhealthy ways, be it over exercising or guilting ourselves if do not workout enough. To be frank with you guys, I absolutely can go weeks without working out or engaging in exercise past walking around the block or hiking. When I am in one of those phases, I focus on living an active life and looking for ways to incorporate movement in my day without carving out time specifically for a workout.

Here are some ideas on how to be more active without putting pressure on yourself to work out:

Take the stairs

Park far from your destination and walk

Walk or bike to anything that is a half a mile or a mile away

Turn on your favorite music and dance while cooking

Add some extra vigor to your cleaning routine

Take walking meetings instead of sitting (Steve Jobs did this)!

Walk around while on the phone

Deliver messages instead of using email or interoffice mail at work

Use the bathroom on a different floor and take the stairs up

Stretch, stand and shake your booty a little bit every hour

Stand at your computer

Hide the remote and get up to change the channel

Adding movement into your day does not need to be this big grandiose event. It can be a simple way to honor what your body can do. All the while celebrating the little victories along the way!

Internal Dialogue

A big focus of this chapter was to address the fact that much of our struggle with food can be wrapped up in a lack of self-love and body-acceptance. If you suspect that part of your struggle with properly nourishing your body is rooted in the way you feel about yourself, I encourage you to make an effort to cultivate more self-love.

If you are not sure where to start, then I recommend trying positive affirmations. A positive affirmation is a statement that we say aloud or write out on paper that is empowering and loving and when said regularly can help stop the self-sabotaging cycle of negative self-talk.

I believe that each thought we have about ourselves has a cause and an effect in determining how we show up each day. And if we choose powerful affirmations that serve us and lift us up, we will slowly but surely start to notice a shift in our lives. We might feel happier, less stressed, be more at ease and organically want to do good unto ourselves and others. This only reinforces the argument that to change our relationship with food, we have to change the relationship with ourselves. Which, surprise..., helps with developing Body Wisdom.

Positive affirmations reinforce self-love and self-care. By telling our bodies that we love them, that they are beautiful, and that we are grateful for all that they do for us, we will organically start to want to treat them kindly. By consciously choosing some empowering thoughts, we can change our actions and be more in tune with our Body Wisdom. And you can do all of this right now, without actually changing anything about your body. Your body is not "right or wrong," it just is the way it is today, so accept it, love it and get on with your day. Chances are you have been hating yourself for a while and I am willing to bet that it has not gotten you the results that you want, so try loving yourself as you are instead.

Tuning Inward

Earlier I mentioned what a dieter's thought process would be if they were thinking of having some bread. If we shift into the mindset of eating for Body Wisdom we might ask ourselves the following:

"Will this bread make me feel energize and nourished?"
"Is it a whole grain bread that is high in fiber and nutrients?"
"Does it have the potential to make me feel sluggish or irritable?"
"Do I truly want the bread and will I enjoy it?"

These questions encourage us to look inward for answers and address the desire to eat in a way that is not overly emotional like that of a dieter. It also has nothing to do with weight or our value as a person. Inquiry like this is woven into intuitive eating and allows us to bring awareness to how our thoughts influence how we eat. While the premise of intuitive eating is to listen to the body for cues, we want to make sure that we don't use the guidelines of "eating when hungry and stopping when full" to create just another *diet-mentality* to operate from.

Creating a Healthy Relationship with Your Intuition

If we view the principles of intuitive eating as hard and fast rules that we must obey, then we find ourselves right back in the throes of a diet mentality. Intuitive eating is a tool to developing Body Wisdom, but how we choose to utilize this tool is where our true power arises. For example, when our body signals that we are hungry, it is nothing more than a piece of information traveling through our system about the state of our blood sugar.

Think of it like an email from our stomach to our brain. We can open the email, process the information, and then choose whether or not we want to act on the instructions. Likewise, if we eat dairy and get sick to our stomach, this is information from our body that we might be lactose intolerant. We can CHOOSE to stop eating dairy if we want, or we can continue to eat dairy despite our upset stomach because, yolo. The key to both of these scenarios is to open yourself up to receiving communication from your body (intuition) but then using your personal power to decide how you are going to act (eat).

We do not want to use the Intuitive Eating model as an excuse to make irrational decisions throughout the day to day nuances of our life either. Let's say we have a busy day at work where we are on site and away from our normal office space that is conveniently a few feet away from the break room where there are always snacks available. On this particular morning, we might wake up and not be hungry for breakfast. While intuitive eating is of course about listening to our body's hunger signals, our body cannot account for the fact that today is not like every other day.

It doesn't know we won't have time to eat for hours and hours because we are on site and not at our desk. But, our rational brain does. So use your brain and eat something anyways so you are not going half the day without eating, or at least plan accordingly and bring some meal prepped food or snacks with you. And if you are out to happy hour with some friends at bar and one orders delicious smelling fries it's totally okay to eat some even if you are not hungry. This is just one example where we need to not live and die by the principles of intuitive eating or turn it into the "hunger and fullness diet" as Isabel Foxen Duke calls it, but rather use these principles as a tool to powerfully set us up for honoring our Body Wisdom.

Another mindset medicine tip I want to explore which is part of intuitive eating and Body Wisdom is understanding the effect our thoughts can have on how we eat. Believe it or not, the thoughts we are having are influencing our behavior around food.

Have you ever found yourself saying that:
"I can't be trusted around (insert specific food)?"

How about... "I know I need to stop eating sugar but I can't seem to stop/control myself." Or "I am addicted to sugar."

Or... "If I could just stop eating bread I'd be good." But then you stuff bread rolls in your mouth?

These types of stories you are telling yourself over and over again are absolutely having an impact on the behaviors you are exhibiting around food. In fact they are all limiting beliefs about yourself that hold you back from developing Body Wisdom and are most likely self-fulfilling prophecies. The good news is that you can change them by choosing more empowering beliefs and telling yourself a different story.

Here are some other stories and thoughts that you can try on for yourself. Repeat them over and over, as much as needed until you truly believe them to be true or make up your own new ones.

"My body is amazing and deserves to be nourished."
"I can have sugar if I want it."
"Carbs are not evil and I can eat them if I want."
"I get to choose what to eat and I deserve to eat the foods I love."
"I want to feel good so I am going to eat what makes me feel vibrant."

Our thoughts are powerful catalysts for action, while we cannot control all of our thoughts we can consciously choose to think some empowering ones! And in my experience this makes a huge difference.

Chapter 8 ACTION STEPS:

Discovery #1: Pick three meals this week and practice intuitive eating. Slow down and ask yourself what it is you want to eat. What sounds appetizing and delicious. Do not base the choice on your food rules, rather what you would actually enjoy eating. Then remove all distractions, phone, TV etc. Before eating, rate your hunger on a scale of one to ten, one being uncomfortably starving and ten being uncomfortably full/ stuffed. Then chew each bite 7-10 times each and rate your fullness while you eat.

Discovery #2: During the three meals pay attention to the smells, taste, texture, colors and how satisfying each bite is. Literally just slow down and get present to eating. Gage your fullness throughout the meal and at the end of it. Write down any observations that you make, i.e. how do you feel mentally, emotionally, physically?

Discovery #3: What conversations do you have with yourself around meal time and around specific types of foods? Consider that you might be participating in a self-fulfilling prophecy and perhaps changing the conversation around these foods might help empower you to behave differently around them. List the beliefs you have about specific food and then tell yourself a more empowering story.

9
BIOLOGY AND EATING PSYCHOLOGY

"Appetite is powerfully influenced by the timing of our meals. If we artificially skip meals, the body will scream for more food. If you struggle with an unruly appetite, be sure to experiment with eating regular meals."

"Eating is Life. Celebrate food, celebrate your good fortune, honor the body, play, and allow yourself to have a beautiful soulful relationship with food"

Psychology of Eating Words of Wisdom

Understanding how our thoughts influence our behavior around food can empower us to upgrade our thinking and in turn upgrade our health and Body Wisdom. But this does not occur in a vacuum. What and how we eat can have a powerful influence on our personality and mood, thus affecting how we show up each day.

You Are What You Eat

As we've previously discussed, the food we eat is ingested into our bodies, metabolized by our digestive system, and then assimilated into the cells that make us who we are. Food, in essence, impacts us as individuals. "You are what you eat" is not only a cliché, but completely true in terms of metabolism and biology. When something enters the digestive system, our bodies begin to break it down by releasing hormones, enzymes and various digestive fluids that break down the food into different molecules that the body can then use (or not use depending on what was consumed) for a variety of metabolic processes. Various nutrients that are supposed to be derived from our food play a huge role in our energy, vibe and disposition about life. It makes sense then that poor-quality food can cause stress, anxiety, mood swings or make us feel depleted since it becomes a part of us through absorption into the bloodstream.

What we eat becomes the fuel for our brain to help operate every systematic function in the body and like a luxury car, it runs best on premium fuel. Eating a wide array of high quality SOUL foods filled with vitamins, minerals, antioxidants and phytonutrients nourish the brain and protect it from inflammation and oxidative stress -- which is caused by free radicals from poor-quality food. When low quality fuel, such as refined and processed foods, are put into our body machine over and over again it does not run optimally. Several studies have found a link between diets high in refined sugar and decreased brain cognition and worsened symptoms of mood disorders like anxiety and depression.[69]

Food and Brain Chemistry

The idea that mood disorders and impairments in brain function are a result of what we eat is a fairly new idea to hit the mainstream. Although it has been studied before, we are only now making this connection and utilizing this information in patient care. I wish that this information was being applied to patients back when I was on depression and anxiety medicines, as it probably would have kept me from being on them in the first place. On the day when I was diagnosed with depression and anxiety, I spent a total of 15-30 minutes with a psychiatrist. I explained my symptoms which included sadness, racing heart, spiraling thoughts, loss of interest in activities or hanging out with friends, sleeping too much and eating poorly. Instead of inquiring about my lifestyle and diet, he was quick to identify my symptoms as depression and prescribe me pharmaceuticals that did nothing but mask the symptoms. This process is SO common amongst those who suffer from depression and anxiety because our medical system is not fully equipped with the knowledge of how lifestyle impacts our brain chemistry.

As I mentioned in a previous chapter, this is a system breakdown in our medical industry as a whole and is not the fault of any individual doctor. While symptoms of depression are easy to identify, understanding why they are caused is more challenging which is why our medical system relies heavily on pharmaceuticals for treatment. Pharmaceuticals *can be* helpful and sometimes necessary but often are not a long-term solution for a lot of people, myself included. What we need to transition into as a society of people who are over-prescribed and under cared for, is a medical approach that works to identify the root cause of what ails us. Functional Medicine, as discussed earlier is an approach to understanding and identifying the source of dis-ease or why it is there in the first place.

The Impact of Stress on Our Biology

Food, nutrition and movement are the primary tools used to help restore the body to full operational capacity. These tools are also essential in combating the stress of living in the fast-paced culture of America. We often assume that our stress is solely caused by external factors such as our job, car, boyfriend, or city. Although stress is a regular response to external circumstances like a hectic schedule, pressures at work or a breakdown in relationships, what we choose to eat or don't eat and how and when we eat are all contributing factors.

While writing this book I followed Whole 30 and discovered that wheat and sugar trigger anxiety for me and after having removed them for 30 days all my symptoms were gone. That was something I did not expect or think was possible. Changing my diet and career had dramatically decreased my anxiety, but there was still this low level baseline from which I lived. When we are providing our body with SOUL food, our response to stressful situations can be altered. Things that once upset us easily might not elicit the same fire alarms, and, in my experience, this reduced stress response can dramatically improve our day to day happiness and overall health in the long run.

Studies have shown that prolonged exposure to stress can be more harmful than smoking.[70] Stress caused by our job, what we eat, our appearance, our commute, and our lack of sleep all add up to create our total stress load. If we are not working to reduce our stress by relaxation techniques, SOUL food, and physical movement, then this extreme amount of stress can become the baseline from which we operate our life. Stress also inhibits our ability to digest our food which often leads to physical discomfort like bloating. This reinforces the fact that the body is a complete system, all parts intimately influencing the whole. Fortunately, what we eat has a direct impact on our stress, attitude and happiness.

Food and Our Mood

There are specific foods that have been shown to increase our stress hormones and influence our mood. Additionally, there are specific nutrient deficiencies that are associated with the prevalence of depression. Although you do not have to avoid these foods by completely flipping your diet on its head, having an awareness of the impact these stress-inducing foods have can help you course correct or make adjustments that can improve your sense of wellbeing.

A couple foods that can contribute to anxiety:

Caffeine: This little guy occurs naturally in coffee, teas, chocolate and is added to a slew of beverages and even packaged foods. Caffeine stimulates our nervous system which can lead to a rapid heartbeat and increase in blood pressure. It's known to cause dehydration which can lead to headaches, and let's be honest, headaches make even the nicest of people a little crabby. Having too much throughout the day or having caffeine too late in the day affects your body's ability to get restful sleep. Sleep is fundamental to health because it is our body's time to regenerate, rest and repair. No one likes a tired child (or adult).

Refined Sugar: Oh dear sugar, how we love you so. Believe it or not, stress is greatly impacted by your blood sugar level. When your blood sugar levels are either too high OR are constantly fluctuating from over consumption, your blood sugar plummets in what is known as a "crash." This blood sugar crash signals to your body to produce cortisol, the stress hormone. When these massive spikes and fluctuations occur repeatedly, adrenal glands continue to release cortisol which signals to your body to pull glucose out of your cells in order to stabilize your blood sugar. Unstable blood sugar can make you feel the same way you might feel when angry, scared or stressed out from a situation happening in your life. Controlling your blood sugar through diet will help you be more resilient to stress in the face of everyday life situations.

Artificial Sweeteners: Diet, sugar-free products and sweetener packets with artificial ingredients have been linked to an increase in depression, a disruption in sleep patterns, headaches and even cancer. Aspartame specifically is associated with everything from migraines, confusion, memory loss, depression, irritability and menstrual problems-all things that can greatly impact our mood. Because these substances are not found in nature our body treats them like toxins.

Alcohol: I love a glass of wine as much as the next girl but alcohol is a depressant and can interfere with our body's ability to produce and utilize our neurotransmitter serotonin, which plays a role in mood stabilization. Not only that but having alcohol late at night to wind down after a tough day can spike your blood sugar levels and lead to dehydration making it difficult to get a good night's sleep which could lead to more anxiety and depression the next day. I still drink alcohol because I enjoy it, but I keep this in mind when I do.

Refined Flour and Gluten: Refined flour and gluten, the protein found in wheat can trigger anxiety, depression and stress in some people. Anecdotally from my own life, I do not have a gluten sensitivity, but when I eat white flour or have certain gluten containing beers, I notice a spike in anxiety either on the same day or the following. Additionally, like refined sugar, refined flour can spike your blood sugar leading to an increase in cortisol production, our stress hormone.

Even though certain foods we are consuming can create a stress response in the body, foods we are NOT eating can also prevent cortisol from being minimized. It might surprise you that nutrient deficiencies are linked to mood swings, depression and anxiety as well. It absolutely surprised me when I first learned about it! Here are some nutrients that are commonly found in SOUL food that help to reduce stress and other mood disorders.

L-Tryptophan — This amino acid is responsible for producing chemical messengers in the nervous system. It is also the key player involved in the production of serotonin — your feel good hormone. A deficiency in this essential amino acid can lead to erratic mood swings and depression.[71] Foods that contain L-tryptophan are soybeans, cocoa, cashews, peas, chicken breast, turkey, salmon, oats, walnuts, brown rice, avocados, winter squash and legumes.

Omega-3 fatty acids — There are two essential fatty acids that are required by the body because we are unable to produce these fatty acids without ingesting food. They are Omega-3 and Omega-6. Omega-6 fatty acids are incredibly prevalent in our food supply because of our heavy use of industrial seed oils such as canola, safflower, soybean oil and sunflower oil. Ideally, we want the ratio of these to essential fatty acids to be 1:1 in order to prevent inflammation from excess Omega-6 fatty acids. It might surprise you to learn that the average American eats a ratio of 20:1 grams of omega 6 to omega 3.[72] This means that we are consuming 20 times the amount of Omega 6 to Omega 3. According to several studies, patients with major to mild depression experienced up to a 50% decrease in symptoms and mood swings when given omega-3 fatty acids compared a placebo group.[73] Although researchers aren't exactly sure why this happens, we do know that it helps protect the bodies serotonin and dopamine levels making it an important tool in helping with depression and anxiety. Great sources include fish oil, salmon, sardines, mackerel, hemp seeds, flaxseed oil, walnuts and dark leafy green vegetables like kale and spinach.

B-Vitamins — This group of vitamins supports nervous system functioning. Not only does stress decrease the levels of B vitamins, but a deficiency in these vitamins also causes more anxiety, fatigue and mood problems. B6 specifically is needed for L-tryptophan to be able to convert into serotonin, an important antidepressant neurotransmitter (it's all connected people). A wide variety of B vitamins can be found in nutritional yeast, fermented foods, animal products like beef or turkey, whole grains, potatoes and bananas.

Magnesium — This nutrient is a powerhouse, and plays a role in some 300+ biochemical enzymatic reactions in the body including the regulation of stress hormones. Studies show that low levels of magnesium are correlated with depression and anxiety.[74] Magnesium may also act as a neuroprotector that is able to modulate the regulation of the blood-brain barrier permeability, which are the regulatory cells between your brain and the rest of the blood in your body. It can also help you sleep by promoting a sense of calm and relaxation. Great sources included spinach, whole grains, watermelon, parsley, paprika, cayenne and if you're really stressed out I love to supplement with CALM brand Magnesium powder.

Vitamin D — Many people are deficient in Vitamin D and there is correlation to low serum levels and increased rates of depression and anxiety disorders. Historically, humans have been able to produce their own Vitamin D from exposing their skin to natural sunlight. In modern day, people either cannot spend enough time outside or wear too many layers and sunscreen to be able to produce all the Vitamin D they need to keep from being deficient. Despite this dilemma, the benefits of sun exposure are still seen even in a clinical setting. For example, one study found that hospitalized patients with depression were discharged more quickly if their room had more natural light.[75] Although the study did not prove that Vitamin D and sunlight was the cause for quicker discharge, there was an undeniable correlation between sunlight and recovery time of patients. It is best to get your Vitamin D from food sources such as fatty fish, eggs, nutritional yeast and from natural sunlight when possible. However, keep in mind that over exposure does increase our risk for some cancers so don't use our need for Vitamin D as an excuse to forgo sunscreen all together or a free pass to sunbathe. Supplementation might also be a good idea- consult with your doctor.

Calcium — Even with all the milk and cheese Americans eat, Calcium deficiency is actually quite common. Calcium is needed for our nervous system to function and low or deficient levels can affect our mood and result in physical symptoms like heart palpitations, tingling sensations and numbness. High levels of calcium are naturally found in organic tofu, almonds, green vegetables and oatmeal.

Given my history with depression and anxiety, I remember how excited I was to learn that changing my diet could majorly impact my mood. In fact, I remember the exact day that I learned Omega-3 deficiency was linked to stress and depression. This information contributed to how I made changes to my diet and lifestyle, and ultimately allowed me to eventually stop taking antidepressants which was very important to me personally. I slowly weaned myself off of the medication and began to apply food as medicine. Over time, my symptoms reduced dramatically, and now I have the ability to be my own doctor and "prescribe" SOUL food (and lifestyle adjustments) for my symptoms instead of using pharmaceutical drugs.

Looking back, it makes me sad to think about how long I wasted believing that I had no control over how I felt, or that I couldn't make diet and lifestyle changes to activate my body's natural healing response. After discovering how nutrient deficiencies contribute to mood stability, I went straight to the store and bought the world's biggest bag of hemp seeds, box of nutritional yeast, flax oil and sauerkraut. I add the hemp seeds and nutritional yeast to almost everything I eat and enjoy a big spoonful of the sauerkraut (for my gut health) every day. It is through the transformational shift in my mental health that took place as a result of the modifications I made to my diet and lifestyle that I believe natural healing is possible for others. Food is powerful medicine that is always at our fingertips, we just have to decide if we are willing to put in the effort to learn how to apply it. This of course requires that food is no longer about weight-loss as well rather about nourishing our body.

Food Mood Cycles and the Backfire of Restriction

Adopting a new lifestyle and figuring out what to eat, how much to eat, and when to eat can drive any person completely crazy. It's part of the reason why yo-yo dieting is a side effect of changing your lifestyle that so many people deal with. Yet learning the psychology of yo-yo dieting and how your body, mind and hunger hormones work can help you ditch the food drama and diets for good.

When I was in high school I tried every diet under the sun to lose weight. Before I fully recovered from my eating disorder, there were many years spent in the recovery process. Often, I would start my day with a nonfat sugar-free vanilla latte and an apple. Lunch would consist of a salad without dressing, meat or cheese, and around 3pm I might have a snack like almonds or another apple. By the time dinner rolled around, I would be so hungry from restricting and monitoring my food intake all day that I would stand in the pantry and literally shove cookies in my mouth really fast while no one was looking.

Meanwhile I'd pop a hot pocket (or three) in the microwave to inhale as if they were oxygen. If I still had room, I'd go to the fridge and eat leftovers right from the container without even bothering to close the door. In recognizing what I had done, I would hate myself for ruining my progress and throw it all up all the while reassuring myself that I would never binge eat again. The issue with promising myself I would never binge again is that I continued to repeat this cycle for nearly a decade. I was a textbook pendulum swinger going from one extreme to the next with no sense of balance or ease around food. I was either "on the wagon or off" as they say.

Although I was able to identify the binge-restrict pattern in my behavior, I found it extremely challenging to mentally break free from the cycle. Even though it is very well scientifically documented that calorie restriction leads to binge eating[76] , like many, I would chalk it up to a lack of willpower and told myself that if I could just find the self-control to contain myself, this problem would disappear. On the contrary, I have discovered that a lack of willpower has absolutely nothing to do with the behavior I was exhibiting. It is a two sided coin with the restrictive diet mentality on one side and our primal biology and nutritional needs on the other. They both heavily influence each other and how and what we eat.

First, Let's Get into the Psychological Mindset Side

When we are consumed by thoughts of food for most of our day, it takes everything in us to not eat an entire box of Goldfish in one sitting and we tend to hide our eating habits out of sight of others so no one can see. This to me makes it obvious that we have a mindset and behavioral problem with how we relate to food, not a willpower problem.

When our first and last thought of the day are about what we ate, what we didn't eat, or if we should have eaten at all, it's damn near impossible to know peace, joy, freedom, love or happiness. It's like a self-inflicted food prison with no window to the outside. When we find ourselves thinking about what we should and shouldn't eat all the while daydreaming about pillow-y soft donuts, we are stuck in the diet-mentality I previously described. And instances of bingeing is what leads us to question the integrity of our willpower, rather than the health of our habits and mindset.

The frustration with our willpower makes us cling to the widely spread false promise that restricting "bad foods" will make us lose weight or fix this problem with food, so we assure ourselves that this won't happen again and we will exhibit the most epic self-control anyone has ever seen. Starting tomorrow...or Monday.

But... it just doesn't work like that because our bodies are more intelligent than our intention of willpower and self-control. There is no amount of either that will stop this cycle from happening again. According to several scientists, like any energy expenditure, we only have a limited supply of willpower each day before we become depleted and can no longer rely on it.[77]

Decision Making Fatigue

Tim Ferriss, a well-known entrepreneur, has a popular podcast that has discussed the idea of "decision making fatigue." In essence, the more decisions we have to make throughout the day the harder it becomes to make decisions that serve our goals as the day progresses. Ever notice how you eat well in the morning but all hell breaks loose at night? Or eat well all week only to throw in the towel come the weekend? This is the result of using our "willpower" to make good decisions, but since it's a limited resource and it gets depleted throughout the course of the day it's not the best tool to use.

This is part of the problem in relying on your self-control to help you accomplish your goals. Even mega-minds in our society such as Steve Jobs recognized that our will power and ability to make sound decisions is limited each day. This is why Steve wore the same jeans and black shirt to work every single day for years. It was one less decision he had to make, and thus a powerful tool for reserving more of his energy for the more complex decisions that truly mattered to him and his success.

The idea that we have a limited capacity to make decisions each day is why having autonomy in our way of eating is helpful and why meal prepping is so popular but also explains why we often don't succeed at diets when it involves restriction and often too many changes at once. We tend to feel like there is something wrong with us or that we are a failure when things do not go according to plan. In reality, this has nothing to do with failure or some kind of character flaw. It could be that we are not setting ourselves up for success and trying to fight against biological urges.

Additionally, I do believe that instead of trying to force things to happen or resist things from happening, we have to look at our underlying desires and commitments to creating change in our life. Accomplishing a goal should not rely on the strength of your will, but rather should depend on the underlying drive or "hunger" for something to be different in your life. When we find it hard to act according to our desired goals, we should instead look inward and investigate what might actually be holding us back and/or driving our behavior. There might be abandoned desires, or inauthentic reasons, that need to be brought to light that "*will* us into action" without actually increasing our utilization of "willpower." (I dive much deeper into this idea later on, so hold that thought).

Normal Eaters Don't Use Willpower

Although it sounds counter-intuitive, we have to let go of the entire idea of controlling ourselves if we want to tap into our Body Wisdom. To help you envision what this looks like, think of the most "normal" rational eater you know. The type of person who eats an appropriate amount of food for their body type, seems to eat whatever they want, stops when they are full and does not seem even the slightest bit controlled by food.

These are the people that often take home leftovers from the restaurant. You know the type. The person who can eat a couple of tacos, or slices of pizza and then be done with it. The person who can eat a cookie, absolutely enjoy it and allow it to be a complete experience. That cookie symbolizes nothing except that they had a cookie and then they can put a metaphorical "period" after eating it. This type of eater may have been eating a little crappy for a couple of weeks and can very casually start to make healthier choices so they feel better without being like "I am a disgusting fat pig. I need to go on a diet."

The core difference between you and the normal eater is **not** willpower but rather a difference in mental framework, as they are not fighting the urge to eat pizza and cookies all day. Generally speaking someone with a normal relationship with food wants to feel good physically so over consuming foods, i.e. eat an entire carton of ice cream in a sitting, would make them feel sick which eliminates the urge to do so. Again they are not using "willpower," there is just no desire to do that and no perceived future deprivation or restriction from dieting (aka diet starts Monday so let's eat the entire pizza right now).

As an anecdote from my personal experience, people are often impressed with my "willpower" and commend me for being so disciplined with the foods that I eat. In hearing this, my response is always the same...it has nothing to do with willpower or discipline.

I do not try to fight myself from having anything if I want it. While I absolutely love french fries, I know that they don't always make me feel the best. It's not that I never eat them, in fact I had them the night before writing the sentence you are currently reading, I just take into account the impact they have on my body (not weight- just the physical discomfort like fatigue) before eating them. I care about feeling good physically and creating vibrancy in my beautiful body machine so I use that lens to look through when choosing whether to eat the fries or not. Same thing goes for kale. I know when I load up on leafy greens I physically feel really good, so my desire to eat them is that much greater. It's not about weight, rather a deep commitment to honoring my body with vibrant foods that lift my vibration higher. Despite what you might think, I am not sitting here ferociously fighting the urge to eat cookies, rather I am deeply connected to my desire to feel good. Plus I completely allow myself to enjoy every bite of cookies when I am eating them. And it's worth mentioning that my body size no longer drives my food choices.

If this is something you struggle with, there are a few fundamental concepts that I want you to take away from this discussion:

First, food is first and foremost nourishment to sustain life, not a mechanism to gain or lose weight. It can be physical or emotional nourishment and while emotional eating gets a bad rap, it's not all that bad. i.e. cake on birthdays or ice cream after a break are both totally ok reasons to eat. Allowing yourself to eat anything without judgement, shame and guilt is what grants us access to the kingdom of food freedom. It's when we judge ourselves that we contribute to an unhealthy relationship with food. If we want to tune into Body Wisdom and develop a nourishing relationship with food then we have to stop judging our ourselves or trying to control our food. We have to be neutral and observe our physical state instead of giving power to our perception of "how we did" with eating.

Second, willpower and self-control are not the answer. Willpower is a limited resource and it will almost always run out. The more we try to fight our urge to eat something (aka have self-control around certain foods) the more likely we are to totally freak out and eat *all the things* when we can no longer fight the urge. Part of the process is giving up total control and just letting your food be what it will be. Do this for long enough and your relationship with it will balance out over time.

Third, remember this: Binge eating is a normal reaction to deprivation and restriction, so by removing the deprivation and restriction, aka the desire to control and use willpower not to eat, reduces the likelihood of binge eating over time. This is how our biology works and that psychology. It literally sets us up for binge eating or "falling off the wagon" when food is scarce.

Stop Restricting

What establishing a healthy relationship with food often boils down to is how we perceive the impact of food on our bodies. When I was obsessed with being thin, everything I ate was either helping or hurting the goal of creating the perfect body. In order to loosen the grip I had on food, or rather food to loosen its grip on me, I had to be less attached to the way I looked. I had to decide that my value and self-worth was independent from the size of my body. I also had to choose my own sanity, ease and peace over trying to shrink my body and I had to do every time I felt the urge to control. It's really moment to moment, a practice that slowly gets easier.

We have to shift our focus away from our physical appearance so that over time our need to control food decreases. Creating this freedom and grace is complex, because human behavior is so multifaceted. Before I set out to change my relationship with food to improve my emotional well-being, I had not considered the impact of my food choices on my physical body. Our body has built-in biological mechanisms that are evolutionarily necessary to ensure that we have all the nutrients available for us to survive. By restricting my calorie intake so much in the morning, I was setting myself up to binge later because I was denying my body the nutrients it needed to perform basic metabolic processes. This next section is about the biological implications that contribute to how, when and what we eat.

The Biology of Deprivation and Hunger Hormones

The drive to binge on food when we restrict ourselves is the way we are hardwired as human beings. When we are calorically deficient, we can easily become nutritionally deficient. This threat to our survival sends our bodies into "fight or flight" mode because they think we are starving. While this may seem frustrating to our ego, our bodies are genius in this way in that this mechanism works to prevent us from dying unnecessarily. Remember, we used to have to chase our food down with spears so this was a very useful aspect of our biology pre Grubhub and Postmates days.

When we restrict food, hunger hormone production increases in our bodies, our blood sugar drops, our cortisol, or stress hormone, spikes and everything in our body tells us to eat. Our body will even increase the amount of pleasure we receive from food to encourage us to eat more so we can survive and not starve to death.[78] Our biology does not know we are on a "diet," or "eating clean" (which I think is wellness culture's term for dieting)" or "are too busy to eat," because it literally thinks there is a food shortage. That's why eating balanced meals throughout the day tells our body that it will survive, and therefore decreases cravings and the drive to keep eating past the point of being comfortably full. So not only do we get psychologically tripped up when we restrict food, but we do biologically as well.

Nutritional Biology

To help you understand what is happening inside your body, here is a Cliff Notes lesson in nutritional biology. Not everyone reading this is a chronic dieter or has an eating disorder but if you struggle with anything related to feeding yourself in a balanced way, understanding how our brain and biology influence our mood and patterns of eating can help get us get closer to Body Wisdom.

Our biology is designed to keep us alive. It's our body's job. By consuming unbalanced meals from a macronutrient standpoint, our biology gets a little twisted. Contrary to popular belief, eating passed the point of being comfortably full (or overeating per say) is not just related to diet culture in America, emotional eating, or binge eating disorders. Overeating can be perpetuated by not managing our appetite and hunger throughout the day. Whether this is intentional or not, under consuming an adequate amount of SOUL food will lead to our biology driving us to eat more.

There are specific mechanisms inside our body that will encourage eating, and this cascade starts with our hormones and blood sugar status. Let's say you skip breakfast for whatever reason, or it consists of coffee or a sweetened almond milk latte and a small amount of food. It's likely that you arrive at lunch pretty dang hungry. Your blood sugar is low, you might be light headed, a little irritable, have brain fog, and be ready to eat every damn thing in site. Perhaps you are able to suppress the drive to eat through lunch and make it to dinner, either way, you are energy (calorie) deficient and you might even feel stressed.

As I previously mentioned, this is because when our blood sugar gets too low our adrenal glands will release our two primary stress hormones called cortisol and adrenaline which signal to the liver to release stored glucose in order to bring our blood sugar back up to normal levels so our brain can function properly.[79] When our blood sugar gets too low our hormones, that are usually managed in a way to prevent excess hunger, become unbalanced. This imbalance creates an excessive amount of stress hormones, which then elevates the levels of neuropeptide y, cholecystokinin[80] and ghrelin which are all hunger-inducing hormones. [81] Additionally, certain foods either activate or deactivate these hunger hormones which tell the brain we are full. If they are not signaled to turn off by the consumption of SOUL foods, then the body makes us crave our fastest-digesting form of fuel to help keep us moving which are simple carbohydrates.

This used to be fruit for early humans but in today's modern world it's white bread, sugar, soda, package snack foods like cookies and chips. This is why we crave them so intensely under times of stress, when we are tired or when we haven't been eating balanced meals. Our biology is just trying to keep our cells and brain working by making you crave foods that will rapidly become fuel for the brain and cells. Makes sense right?

When we do not utilize our first and second meal of the day to balance our blood sugar, we start our morning off with added stress and low blood sugar, which is a hormonal cocktail for making certain food choices for the rest of the day and eating past the point of being comfortably full later on. It's why we often make bad decisions by the time lunch or dinner rolls around, because our bodies are literally screaming for calories and quick fuel. It's also why dinner is often people's biggest meal of the day or is followed by a continually stream of snacking or binge eating.

It's not that our biology is out to get us. It just doesn't know that we are intentionally or unintentionally restricting calories, or that we forgot to eat, or that we are not making time for breakfast or eating a balanced meal from a macronutrient standpoint of protein, healthy fat, fiber and carbohydrates.

Seriously, your body does not know the difference between a famine and a crash diet, so even though your intentions are to lose weight, your body just wants to stay alive and be fed. By the time we get home after a day of not eating balanced meals, our body is so nutritionally deficient and hormonally hungry (maybe not physically hungry because you did eat something) that you eat everything in your pantry or you eat so much that you become uncomfortably full.

Instead of acknowledging that the food choices made throughout the earlier parts of our day clearly did not serve our biology by balancing our hunger hormones, we instead turn to shame and guilt while blaming our lack of will-power. This sets us up to believe that we can simply vow to never binge/overeat again because we are still relying on our willpower to control our eating habits. However, overeating the day before will likely reduce our appetite the next morning which makes us more likely to skip meals or eat less than we might need first thing, restricting until later and the pattern continues.

It's Not Willpower, it's Neuroscience

Can you see how these seemingly common actions of skipping meals, eating past the point of fullness, and not eating adequate amounts of vital macronutrients contributes to this vicious cycle? This entire process of making our bodies "earn" our food actually slows down the metabolism, which makes you more likely to gain weight when the original intention was often to do the opposite.

Our biology and metabolism will always adjust to the amount of energy we are providing it with. When we repeatedly start our day without food, arrive at lunch starving day in and day out, and do a poor job of managing balanced blood sugar, our body slows down the metabolism in an attempt to keep us alive.

"Eat less, and you will lose weight."

That's what we've been told, right? But again, eating at too great of a caloric deficit throughout the day can cause the hormones that control your appetite to go haywire.

According to neuroscientist, Dr. Sandra Aamodt, author of the book Why Diets Make Us Fat, the root of our problem with dieting and maintaining weight loss is not a willpower problem, rather a neuroscience problem.[82] Our brain will have our body adjust to the amount of food we consume, so dramatically reducing your calories during the day when your metabolism is most active ultimately sets you up for binge eating at night, a slower metabolism and potentially a higher set-point weight overtime.

Weight set-point theory explains the built in control system that dictates the weight at which our body runs optimally. In essence our body has a predetermined weight at which it wants us to be at to be healthy, whether or not society and your doctor agrees. It is part of our weight regulation system and runs like a thermostat.[83] . Our body will work very hard to keep us within this weight range which is why long term weight loss from dieting does not work. Some people naturally have a higher set point while others have lower set points (or temperatures on a thermostat per say). This explains why two people can eat very similarly and have very different body sizes and weights.

I am sure we all have a friend who eats whatever they want and maintains a smaller body- say hello to our bodies weight regulation system or set-point. We know now that calorie restriction turns on the bodies fat storing mode as a protective measure from starvation, and increase in our set-point, which is why the initial success of dieting is followed by a plateau and then often weight regain.

Relying on calorie restriction is outdated science and has been proven to not work.[84] We now know this. So the question becomes, "how do we use nutrition to help decrease our chances of bingeing and to have more sanity when eating?"

Here are my top tips for having a balanced relationship with food and nourishing your body:

1. Eat balanced meals at least 3 times a day. I recommend having the amount of food you eat for breakfast resemble the amount you eat for lunch and dinner. (personally. I am not a huge snacker but if you need an afternoon snack look for a SOUL-food one).

   Many people's consumption of food throughout the day is shaped like a cone. The tiny, narrow part in the morning and the wider base at the bottom. The goal is to get our day looking like a tube or pipe. Each meal containing similar amounts of quality sources of carbohydrates and fiber from vegetables, healthy fat and protein. If one meal is too be larger than the others make it lunch, which is when our metabolism is at its best. This is not about losing weight, rather what will make you feel your best because of balanced blood sugar.

2. Don't let yourself get "hangry"

   Hunger should never be an emergency, it should be a gradual sensation of a readiness to eat. Whenever you experience moments of being "hangry" this is a good indication that your blood sugar is not being very well-managed. This is not an error or mistake on your part, but a good indication that your body did not get enough healthy fats, protein, and fiber. To prevent this from happening again, set an intention to make your next meal well-balanced. Also if you find yourself not feeling full then we might be responding to emotional hunger or dehydration. Again, we want to listen to and interpret the information our body sends us, this is Body Wisdom.

3. Monitor how much food you need to eat at breakfast to stay satiated until lunch and then again to dinner.

   For example, try varying amounts of food at breakfast and monitor how long it takes you to feel hungry for lunch. If you feel hungry an hour after breakfast, you most likely did not eat enough! Meals should keep you energized and satiated until your next opportunity to eat or around 3-5 hours. If you feel unsatisfied an hour or two after eating breakfast, try adding more healthy fats, protein, and fibrous carbohydrates from vegetables.

AND- keep in mind that some days you might be hungrier than others, and that's perfectly okay. HONOR THAT! It's part of Body Wisdom.

When we feed our body high quality SOUL food in a quantity that is appropriate for our body size, we begin to feel more balanced mentally and physically around food. Something I have seen as a nutrition and health professional over the years is how both the physiological and biological effects are looked at in isolation, but our body is a system where everything is connected.

In order for this nutritional information to not be interpreted like a diet you have to look at it from a weight neutral standpoint, meaning gaining or losing weight is not good or bad, weight is just weight, body size is just body size. We have to eat in a way to honor ourselves, again coming from that place of self-care.

Embracing a "holistic mindset" when considering how our mental framework towards eating and our choices impact our hormones, blood sugar balance, mood, energy, and even our digestive system is incredibly important in learning how to act on the signals your body is sending you.

Chapter 9 ACTION STEPS:

Discovery #1: For the next 3 days every time you eat look for the following on your plate: Fiber and carbohydrates from vegetables. This includes broccoli, leafy greens, cauliflower, sweet potatoes, zucchini etc.

Healthy fat from coconut oil, nuts, seeds, olives, avocado or olive oil, and protein from eggs, meat, fish, tofu, or beans.

Discovery #2: After 3 days of eating balanced meals, evaluate how you feel. Are you more grounded? More stable? More clear-headed? Really compare how you normally feel to how you now feel eating balanced meals.

Discovery #3: Practice having no food restrictions for the next 3 days. If you want a cookie, have a cookie. If you want nachos instead of a salad, order the damn nachos. Try letting yourself have what you want without deprivation or restriction. Be sure to enjoy the food.

Discovery #3: After 3 days of practicing no food restriction, notice how you feel. Do you feel more free? More relaxed? Are you noticing old desires for food starting to shift?

10
F*CK THE NUMBERS

"It's true, the scale can only give you a numerical reflection of your relationship with gravity. That's it. It cannot measure beauty, talent, purpose, life force, possibility, strength, or love. Don't give the scale more power than it has earned."

—Steve Maraboli

With my newly developed awareness of the powerful implications our food choices have on our health and biology, I became passionately driven to apply this knowledge to my entire life. The intense pull from within me to transform my own health made my purpose in life very clear, so I decided to go back to school to become a health coach and study nutrition.

After relinquishing my responsibilities as a restaurant chef-owner in 2017, I decided to offer some personal chef services to clients on the side while I was taking my nutrition classes. It was a campaign to support people in changing their lives through the idea of food as medicine. Over the course of a couple weeks I designed a beautiful menu, multiple meal packages, and figured out a delivery schedule with sustainable packaging. Then I blasted the news out through every possible channel.

The offerings included a variety of meals from comforting classics like lasagna to cell nourishing watercress and kale salads. The premise was very much in alignment with my ethos and philosophy that when we consume SOUL food we do not have to be mindful of much else because our bodies know what to do. Our hormones balance out, the immune system bolsters up, our weight normalizes for our body type and we end up feeling good in the process. Eating SOUL food is a single action that has an effect on every system in the body and how we show up in life, and it was my newly declared duty to start to help others experience this transformation.

With all of my preparation and experience, the response to my Private Chef services was lackluster to say the least, so I enrolled my dad in the hopes that he might get some of his cigar lounge buddies on board. Sure enough, a handful of men in their 40's thru 70s agreed to give me a shot. Naturally this excited me as all of them were dealing with body ailments that I knew would mellow out with proper nutrition and food. Some had high blood pressure, hypertension, diabetes and (not surprising to me) all of them wanted to lose some weight. The effects of years of eating a SAD diet and trying to diet had physically taken a noticeable toll on these men, and I was thrilled to be applying my passion for food as medicine to help others heal.

Unfortunately, that thrill wore off almost instantly. My enthusiasm for high-vibe food that would flood the body with nutrients was quickly diminished once my clients began to voice concern about calories and macro counts for carbohydrates, fats, and protein. Everyone wanted low-calorie, low carb, high protein, low-fat meals that they believed would help them lose weight and get healthier. While unbeknownst to these men that there was new science that explained not all calories are created equal, they were resistant to my pleas to not seek calorie and macro counts but stay focused on the fact that they were eating 100% real food their body recognized. As hard as I tried, I couldn't sway them from the notion that counting calories was the key to weight loss and longevity. This very dogmatic principle was first popularized in the early 1900's and up until recently had been continually reinforced by health professionals, food companies and media outlets.

Simple As Calories In Calories Out, Right?

Naturally we assume, because of what we have been told, that in order to lose weight we have to eat less. The idea of energy balance as it has been described is pervasive in society in part because it's easy to understand and in *theory* makes sense as "calories in vs calories out" adheres to the basic laws of thermodynamics. We now know that the calorie balance equation is not that simple, and the body treats calories differently based on the source. For example 100 calories of Oreos is not the same as 100 calories of broccoli for a variety of reasons. The Oreos are devoid of fiber yet rich in simple carbohydrates, processed vegetable oils and sugar that spike your blood sugar, whereas the broccoli is high in phytonutrients, vitamins and fiber that helps keep your blood sugar balanced and nourishes the body on a cellular level. Same amount of calories, dramatically different biological impact which blows the reliability of the calorie theory out of the water.

Granted, when the calorie theory was established centuries ago, humanity didn't have fast-food, Oreos, or low-calorie packs to confuse the usefulness of calories when thinking about how our metabolism functions. The origin of "the calorie" dates back to as early as 1819 when Nicole Clement, a French chemist, lectured about steam engines in Paris. It was first used as a unit of heat where a single calorie is a unit of energy that increases the temperature of a gram of water by a single degree Celsius.[85] Later in 1887 Wilbur Olin Atwater, an American chemist, revolutionized our idea of what a calorie meant. He worked for the United States Department of Agriculture (USDA) and began researching the energy content of various foods. He did this by burning different types of food in a what is called a *bomb calorimeter* where the amount of heat given off by a food determines its calorie content. Based on the heat and ash left behind, Atwater was able to determine how much energy, i.e. calories, were in individual food items. This information was used by the USDA to outfit the first ever database of food composition that would affect future nutritional education in our country.[87] The experiment created a concrete yet practical link between food and energy that Americans were quick to grasp onto.

The idea that all you had to do to lose weight was to burn off more energy, or heat, than you consumed is easy to conceptualize. The average American now had a clear rationale for how to manage their diet and exercise routines. Given the sheer simplicity of counting numbers, something any person over the age of seven (7) could do, calorie counting became a popular phenomenon. At face value counting calories made sense. However this overwhelming consensus to accept the reliability of calorie-counting for weight loss lead to our obsession of controlling weight by restricting our calorie intake. This rigid framework began to develop into a belief that foods low in calorie, regardless of their nutritional value, were somehow healthy from a biological standpoint. This concept paved the way for food companies to proclaim their products were healthy because they were low in calories. This marketing infiltrated the minds of us all and resulted in a morality crisis, as foods were now seen as good or bad based on their calorie count.

The alluring element of control that counting calories provides is also its pitiful downfall and almost by design, the explanation was bound to fail. Overtime, nutrition researchers began to learn more about the complicated biological mechanisms that take place in the body when we consume all types of food and food-like things. Given that we used to think the world was flat and also the center of the universe, it's easy to understand that the science of calorie and energy expenditure was, at the time, incomplete. In reality, the calorie content of food has far less of an impact on our health and weight when compared to the source, quality, and nutrient concentration of what we eat.

Weight Loss Culture and Popular Fad Diets

Unfortunately, the concept of weight control through the *"calories in* vs. *calories out"* method lead to well-intentioned people hurting their metabolism in the long run by restricting their food intake and putting their body in "flight or fight" mode. As we talked about in the last chapter, limiting our food intake sets off a chain reaction of several biological mechanisms that lead to our brain telling our body to slow down, use less energy and store more fat. It also shows little regard for the implications of certain foods on our hunger hormones and gut bacteria. Yet the common thread woven between several of the world's most popular diets, be it The Zone Diet, Atkins, Weight Watchers and the recently more popular *If It Fits Your Macros,* is to reduce the nutritional value of food down to a numerical value in order to lose or manage weight. Often not distinguishing between source or quality of ingredients.

All of these diets recommend some form of counting that often results in an obsessive relationship with food where every meal is like balancing a checkbook and judging our performance with food.

The Zone diet promotes a ratio of 40/30/30 for protein, fat and carbohydrates.

The Atkins Diet limits the grams of carbohydrate you can have a day.

Weight Watchers assigns a point value to every food on the planet and allows dieters to only consume a certain number of points per day.

While some of these weight loss protocols do encourage participants or "dieters" in the program to reach for more nutritionally dense SOUL foods they also slightly encourage processed foods too. Ultimately the power is in the hands of individuals. Similar to Weight Watchers, *If It Fits Your Macros* is a structure that gives each person a different amount of macronutrients (macros) which are fats, carbs, and protein in grams that must be tracked daily.

Users of IIFYM can consume a set amount of the three macronutrients in a given day by counting grams of each macronutrient as opposed to choosing food based on the nutritional content, source, quality or how they will make them feel physically. This structure is very popular within the fitness crowd as it allows the individual to "indulge" in previously sworn-off foods such as ice cream, donuts, and cheeseburgers so long as the macronutrient content of these foods fit into the daily macronutrient allotment for protein, fats, and carbs. While this way of eating is helpful for athletes such as bodybuilders to achieve a very specific body composition for competitions, I don't believe this degree of specificity is necessary for the average American who is trying to eat healthfully and not be obsessed with food.

Quality Over Quantity Always

At the core, these programs all focus on the *amount* of food rather than the *quality* of food, which in my opinion promotes the pervasive and damaging *diet mentality*. It literally just sucks the joy out of life and is based on the idea that there is such a thing as a "right and wrong" amount of food to eat. As opposed to using the body's hunger and fullness signals to determine how much to eat for ourselves we let the outside world tell us. As I described earlier, approaching health through the lens of a diet results in an unbalanced relationship with the way we eat, inhibits our ability to develop Body Wisdom, can lead to us eating nutritionally void foods as a backfire of restriction instead of pleasure, and can wreck our metabolism through nutritional starvation. Plus constantly controlling our food intake takes a toll on our enjoyment in life.

With this being said, not all nutrition programs are inherently ill-intentioned. In fact, neither Weight Watchers or IIFYM have "off limits food", where the Zone, Atkins, and several other popular diets do. Removing the "good food vs. bad food" framework is a transformative shift that must occur if we are ever going to loosen our grips on control and eat with sanity as a result of being connected to Body Wisdom.

Eliminating the mindset that there is a "right way and a wrong way to eat" is a foundational shift that needs to occur first in order to nourish your body through intuitive eating and Body Wisdom. The idea that foods are inherently good or bad infuses guilt and shame in the act of eating, which almost always results in negative emotion-driven eating and bingeing. Any effort to restrict or control our consumption of the "off-limits foods" sets us up for obsessive thoughts about them.

Establishing a Positive Relationship with Food

A healthy diet and lifestyle should be one that first and foremost prevents chronic disease and makes you feel vibrant each day, but also supports a healthy relationship with food as a means to nourish your body and bring satisfaction to your life. Establishing a positive relationship with food that also truly makes you feel good requires a shift in how you approach feeding your body. It all depends on your frame of mind, where you are along your journey, and how you define "health" as an individual.

This shift in how you encounter food first requires that you understand the way in which you encounter your diet, which can be confusing given the million ways in which this word has been used in health culture. When we use the word "diet", we are actually referring to a broad spectrum of definitions that have zero absolute truths and cover a diverse range of ways to feed your body. Diet can be used to describe either a prescribed way of eating, i.e the Paleo diet, or it can be used to describe the foods that you typically consume in your daily life. If you tend to jump from one prescribed way of eating to another and find yourself turning down foods that your body legitimately yearns for simply because the "diet" you are on doesn't allow certain foods, then to some degree you are still living in a *diet mentality*. Plus any type of counting, tracking, monitoring, or restricting also means you are dieting. Denying yourself the opportunity to establish the ability to differentiate what foods work best for your body (*your* unique diet) vs what foods are allowed on a "diet", can set you up for an over-analytical approach to food, which ultimately can set you up for a future of an unhealthy obsession with choosing the "right" foods, thus inhibiting true Body Wisdom.

As someone who had an eating disorder, I eventually found solace from the obsession by shifting my focus from "being skinny" to truly just wanting to be sane and healthy. For me personally, this meant deciding that I was worthy of my own love and educating myself on the nutritional content of different foods, our food system, environmental impact, animal rights and food politics so that I was routinely choosing the most nutrient dense foods and eating in a way that made a difference in the world and not just my individual health and weight. At the time, I had never read about food outside of the world of weight loss, so it was truly powerful for me to learn the other complexities of it. With that said, choosing food based exclusively on the nutritional content can lead to another form of disordered eating we are coming to know in our society called Orthorexia, or an unhealthy obsession with the purity of food.

Orthorexia is where restrictive eating from a disordered mentality combines with an obsession over control and results in a fear-based approach to eating. Orthorexia can make an individual afraid to eat certain foods if they are unsure of the origin, preparation method, and "purity." This fixation can be exacerbated in the current climate of nutrition when conflicting data and opinions are the norm. What's unfortunate is that Orthorexia stems from a well-intended goal of consuming high quality food, but the fear-based approach is a recipe for ultimate food restriction and disordered eating.

With so many disordered patterns of eating prevalent in our society, the timeliness of developing true Body Wisdom presents the opportunity to rise above these patterns that are ultimately restricting your growth as an individual. You have been exposed to so many new concepts around foods that feed *dis-ease*, how to fuel your body machine, and how to relinquish a controlling mindset on food. It is so important that you understand where you are at in your journey to Body Wisdom so that you can reflect on the food patterns from your past, but also develop a road map based on positive changes moving forward. My hope in sharing different theories about nutrition with you is to help you to approach making change in your own life that is in no way triggering of painful past experiences. Just like there is not one right way to eat, there is not one right way to view food.

My mission is not to discourage others from trying a "diet" or to make those who are currently on one feel that they have made a wrong decision. My mission is simply to offer up my personal experience of finding Body Wisdom and rising above the restrictive mindset of an eating disorder. The argument I hear most from people who love these types of prescribed and planned lifestyles that entail counting food is that they don't feel like they're on a diet because they are allowed to eat "*non diet-type foods*" such as donuts, french fries, and potato chips. The freedom and flexibility leaves them feeling like their living a lifestyle that is sustainable and supports their health and fitness goals. Perhaps these programs are just a stop along the road on the way to true food freedom and Body Wisdom where you eventually no longer need guidelines, macro counts or points but can truly tune into your body's signals and fully trust yourself around food.

The structure of counting food or looking at it as a set of numbers is not inherently wrong. If you are eating nourishing foods, and also enjoying the foods you love from time to time (like a donut), because *it fits your macros* then by all means party on. If you are not obsessive, compulsive, and crazy, then do you. However, if your goal is to learn to eat intuitively without needing to count macros, grams, points or calories, utilizing the framework of a structured program such as IIFYM or Weight Watchers goes against the grain of intuitive eating because it's not intuitive, it's counting. Your not listening to your body your using your mind. If using this approach is the only way you know how to eat the foods you love, at what point are you able to stop counting and just eat in a way that honors your body's needs and wants?

The sole premise of almost all diet programs out there be it NutriSystem, SlimFast, Jenny Craig, Weight Watchers or IIFYM, is *weight loss* and that is intrinsically where my adversity to them lives. The pursuit of health is not the same pursuit as weight-loss. The pressure to lose weight, while can sometimes (but rarely) be medically necessary, is overwhelmingly the result of our *diet culture* and pervasive body shaming society. We live in a world that has put so much emphasis on people to fit into a single ideal standard of beauty and health.

When our sole reason for eating a certain way is to lose weight, manage our weight or manipulate the way our bodies look, we will be stuck in the vicious cycle of a *diet mentality*. We are constantly being sold this lie that if we just follow *this way of eating* we will be able to look like *this and have that body*. For many of us that is not ever going to be the case, no matter how hard we try we may never look like a supermodel.

A Healthy Weight At Every Size

While I am not here to be the food police, I find it irresponsible to tell people that all foods are created equal in terms of their implication on the health of our bodies, which is exactly what IIFYM does. A direct quote from the website at the time of writing this says *"the foods you choose to eat do not make you fat. Yup, fat loss is 100% not about the foods you eat."* To make sure the context is not misunderstood, what they mean is it's about the amount of food from a macronutrient standpoint that is responsible not the quality or source of the food. While I understand that 1 gram of fat has 9 calories whether it's from canola oil or an avocado, ignoring the distinction between the quality of the fatty acids and nutrient content has implications for the health of our body (and the planet) that clearly are being ignored with this approach. For example, I've previously mentioned that canola oil is a processed oil that is high in Omega-6 fatty acids. It has become known as an inflammatory fat linked to nearly all disease, while avocado is high in unsaturated fat and has far reaching benefits that include the ability to lower LDL, or bad" cholesterol, support brain and cellular health, and helps to keep us feeling full.[87] This examples brings me back to my point that evaluating food based solely on its macro content or point value is just one more way in which we are trying to systematize our way to a socially dictated "health and weight" status based on the physical appearance of our bodies. I believe that the idea of a *healthy weight* as we are taught by our society and medical system is completely false. While popular diets have been prescribed by our "health culture" to force everyone's body into an idealized shape and stature by counting the numbers in our food, our medical system has its own form of classifying "health" based solely on the numbers of our body metrics. Even the medical tools we use to determine what a "healthy weight" is are completely misleading and mostly incorrect. This is where we begin to see an even deeper level of how our society believes health only looks one way, one size, and one shape contributing to disordered relationships with food and an obsession with weight loss *in the name of health* that perverts our ability to develop Body Wisdom.

For example, the Body Mass Index (BMI) is the current gauge our medical system uses to determine if someone is healthy or not based on their weight and height. By definition, the BMI is a weight-to-height ratio, calculated by dividing one's weight in kilograms by the square of one's height in meters. BMI has been used for decades as an indicator of obesity, being overweight, having a healthy weight, or being underweight. The problem is that weight does not necessarily correlate to the health of a person. Although overweight people can be at risk for certain diseases, thin ones can too, and weight is only one piece of the puzzle. Simply using weight as the main metric for health encourages *fatphobia*, disordered eating, body shaming and the pervasive influence of diet culture stemming from our medical system and society at large.

For example, let's compare person A with person B. Person A might have a "healthy BMI" of 22, and look healthy to the outside world based on their body size. Yet Person A routinely consumes fast food, processed food-like stuff, and does not exercise regularly. Turns out Person A has a fast metabolism that is maintained by their brain's "set-point" that keeps them in this "healthy weight range." Just by looking at the size of their body, it would seem that they fit into our systematic box of being "healthy." Person A is also often fatigued, inflamed, irritable and sluggish. Their inability to run a mile without stopping would indicate poor cardiovascular health, which is a more reliable predictor of future heart and health problems as opposed to BMI alone.[88] However, given their lean appearance, and social and medical acceptance of being a "healthy weight", Person A has yet to feel inclined or been pressured by a medical professional to switch up their diet by consuming more nutrient dense foods. Ultimately, this pattern could result in health issues down the line from nutritional deficiencies that were missed through the utilization of BMI and our society's idea of what health looks like.

Now consider person B. This individual is considered by our medical system and society to be "overweight and unhealthy" with a BMI of 27. However, this person has cardiovascular fitness because they can run 2 miles without having to stop, and is showing no signs of chronic disease or illness. Person B is inspired to take care of their health by eating real foods daily and regularly cooking their meals from scratch with SOUL ingredients. Their brain has a higher "set point" or body weight at which it determines it is comfortable and can run optimally. Unfortunately, because of our society's limited mindset of what "healthy" can look like, we view Person B as unhealthy and praise Person A for their lean appearance. Person B might have even been told to lose weight by their doctor regardless of the fact that they are by every valuable measure, a healthy individual. This pattern of determining a person's health based solely on their body metrics is the norm in our culture.

Health is not one body shape, size, or weight. Health is a spectrum of body types, none of which should be more desirable than the others. Weight is just a number, but health is how you choose to nourish, move, and honor your Body Wisdom, not just the foods you eat but how you live your life as well.

Why Thinness Does Not Correlate with Health

Collectively, we have erroneously linked weight to health in a way where well-intentioned doctors, experts, and health and fitness professionals pervert our relationship to our bodies and to food. This has- in many ways, made people in bigger bodies feel stigmatized and like there is something wrong with them because they don't fit into our society's mold of "health." This omnipresent opinion that health doesn't occur at every size, shape or weight has undoubtedly contributed to our country's weight gain and our obsession with dieting and weight loss as a means to attain health.[89] Consequently, it also affected my ability to get the help I needed for my eating disorder. Although I sought treatment twice, my parents and therapist at the time were convinced that I didn't have a severe enough of a problem to need rehab because I was "not thin enough." i.e. not *anorexic-looking* enough. As if an eating disorder is purely based on someone's size and not their mental health and wellbeing. I was reassured that my desire to be thin was just a normal part of growing up. "All girls worry about their weight," was the assertion given, like routine starving, binging and purging was a rite of passage for American girls (or girls in general). Which is absolutely a systematic and cultural problem that is hurting so many people.

At no fault to my parents, they weren't negligent by any means, they just didn't know. My therapist at the time, who is licensed professional, also was just using the knowledge she had. We are systematically taught to determine people's health based on their size. Plus, education and care for those with mental illness, which in my opinion is the root of disordered eating (a mindset issue), is still in many ways in its infancy in our country. It's part of the reason why the discovery of the role our multifaceted gut bugs have on brain health is so alluring and important. But, this pervasive idea that your body's appearance indicates the degree of internal health encourages individuals to focus more on their appearance and less on how they actually feel. In other words, our focus on looking a certain way has taken us out of our bodies and therefore diminishes our Body Wisdom. The emphasis is no longer on how we feel, but solely on how we look.

It is the metric we so often use to determine our self-worth, and this consequently makes us feel like victims to our size and fuses our value as a person to a number on the scale or size of our jeans. Just like how the calorie content of food is not an accurate representation of the nutritional value, our number on the scale is an unreliable representation of our health and worth. Yet so many people constantly weigh themselves and let that number influence how the day is going to go. Instead of checking in with our body and how we are feeling we decide to attempt to "hold ourselves accountable" by getting on the scale or judging ourselves based on the number.

The problem with obsessing over what we weigh is that it feeds our obsession with food. The two do not occur in a vacuum, rather feed off of one another. And while I understand the argument for weighing ourselves as a way to keep us on the hook for making healthier choices, it's simply not the case. Chances are you have been weighing yourself for years and are still not happy with your body so there goes that argument completely. Rather, we are perpetually held hostage by the scale and using the number as a barometer for far too many areas of our life.

It might be a wildly unpopular opinion, but I truly believe that there is more to life than having a "healthy" weight as dictated by society. Fixating on a specific number does not correlate with a happier life. I know this because I am heavier now than I used to be and so much healthier and happier. Despite what it might seem like, I am not anti-weight-loss or against people wanting to look and feel their best, but letting our weight influence how we feel does not result in better habits, a more fulfilling life, or a better relationship with food and our body.

The repercussions of getting on the scale is that we now eat as a response to the number instead of what our body is signaling for. Just one more way external stimulus stunts our ability to develop Body Wisdom by decreasing our connection to hunger and satiety signals and to the information our body is telling us. Eating in reaction to how much our body weighs or what it looks like is not an intuitive process, and it has no regard for the fact that our weight can fluctuate from the minutiae of everyday life. Eating, drinking, urinating, having a bowel movement, exercise, even the freaking weather and a slew of other factors all can influence how much our physical body weighs on any given day. Weighing ourselves literally just makes us feel crappy about our behavior and our body. Truthfully, we don't need to get on the scale to know if we've been eating in a way that honors ourselves or not.

Judgement based on the size of our body or our weight leaves no room for freedom. We trap ourselves in food prison where food and weight has the power to dictate our actions, emotions and sense of well-being. We then allow food to determine if we have been good or bad.

The focus is shifted back into a similar morality crisis because we decide if *we* have been good or bad based on this number.

Just how counting calories or solely focusing on weight-loss truly shifts the focus from wanting to deeply nourish our bodies to wanting to fit ourselves into a predetermined definition of "health", weighing ourselves similarly strips us of our ability to be objective with how we truly feel. Just like how we can ask ourselves if the food we are eating is SOUL or SAD, we can also wake up in the morning and ask ourselves if we are feeling energized, positive and excited to take on the day and do the things we love. We can also wake up and ask ourselves if we are hungry or not. This is truly a more reliable measure of health and well-being that strengthens our connection to Body Wisdom as opposed to stripping us of our self-worth by stepping on the scale or counting our food.

There is an intuitive nature to approaching your lifestyle this way, and counting as it relates to food is *counterintuitive* by its very nature. My hope is for you to be effortlessly and mindlessly healthy. Not counting each piece of food you put in your mouth or over-analyzing even the slightest fluctuation in weight.

Below are some helpful mindset shifts to leave you feeling powerful and strong in both your relationship to food and to your Body Wisdom.

- ▶ The only thing to count is ingredients
- ▶ Exercise is a celebration of what my body can do, not a punishment for what I ate
- ▶ Eating whole foods is not going on a diet, it's taking action to create a transformation in my life and nourish my body deeply.
- ▶ What's important is not how I look, but how I feel
- ▶ It's impossible to get new results with old ways of thinking, doing or being.

Chapter 10 ACTION STEPS:

Discovery #1: Take this opportunity to think of all the ways you think about your health, including what you eat. What "truths" do you tell yourself about eating well, exercising and dieting? What comes to mind when you think about eating salads, vegetables, and whole grains. Does it sound limiting, disgusting, nourishing? What do you tell yourself about drinking alcohol, eating sugar or hitting up the drive thru? Whether subconsciously or consciously, our body can hear our thoughts and it impacts our actions.

Discovery #2: Do you have self-limiting beliefs that sabotage your health? What are they? For example "I am not good enough because I don't look like XYZ." Or "I am not healthy because I am not a size XYZ."

Discovery #3: What is a more powerful thought or way of describing health that you could replace your old thoughts with that will serve your higher self and ultimately your wellness goals.

For example: I am whole and complete the way I am. I am beautiful as I am. Or my measure of health is how I feel not how I look. I wake up with energy, vitality and excitement for the day. My brain is clear and focused. These are all far better measures of health then body size.

11
THE ART OF LASTING LIFESTYLE CHANGE

"Motivation is a nice thing. It's like a warm bath. You want to take one, but it's not enough"

—Tony Robbins

U nderstanding how calorie counting, macro tracking, and obsessing about your weight all operate in stealing joy from your life you can also see that they ultimately distract you from the goal of creating Body Wisdom too. In essence they all make you too tuned into your mind and the outside world, and not enough into your own body. Plus those were all tools designed by diet culture to sell products and contribute to the ever profitable diet, weight loss and "health" industries. Our bodies and what we eat does not need to be so calculated and measured.

Now that you know what is *not* empowering you to get in touch with the wisdom of your body, and the foods that offer the most nutrition per bite, we can talk about the changes that will enable you to establish a solid relationship with your body and how to nourish it. While there are many facets of this process, many of which we have explored, our *mindset, behavior,* and *actions* are just as important. The next two chapters explore these elements more deeply.

Diet and Wellness Culture

As a society, we have been told a massive lie from diet (and sometimes even modern "wellness") culture. Everywhere we look, messages of the "perfect diet" and fast results are coming at us. There is always a new skinny tea, diet pill, way of eating (recently its Keto), herbal supplement or weight loss super food to try. It's no wonder we are often seduced by the idea and belief that changing our health and the shape of our body is borderline instant. The alluring promise of so many diets, health and wellness products, and trends is that specific results are available within specific and often short time frames.

Most humans gravitate towards measurable metrics such as pounds reduced, or inches lost. Comically, you will notice that these metrics yield great results from the marketing efforts of various weight loss companies. I am sure you will not be surprised to learn that the largest diet companies in the world use seductive metrics in their marketing campaigns. At the time of writing this, Jenny Craig's website says "lose up to 16 pounds in just 4 weeks." South Beach Diet's site proclaims you can "lose up to 9 pounds and 3 inches in your first two weeks." And then we have the ultra-extreme HCG diet, that limits calorie intake to 500 per day and promises a weight loss of 1-2 pounds per day.[90] I mean, that shit is cray.

Dieting is the Fast Track to Weight Gain

The outrageous piece to this equation that most dieters don't realize is that diets end up making us gain more weight in the long run. Statistically speaking, the best way to gain weight is to try to lose it by going on a diet.[91] [92] This is because we have biological evolutionary mechanisms in place to help keep our bodies alive that are activated by restrictive diets that advertise massive amounts of weight loss in a short amount of time.

When we restrict food, our metabolism slows down and the body kicks into fat storing mode to help keep us alive. This was very useful when food shortage and famine was a regular part of human life (hello, we used to have to chase down our food with spears remember), but not so handy in the modern world where food can be delivered by touching a few buttons on our smartphone. These mechanisms also encourage our bodies to put on weight after a period of food restriction because our biology, for most of human existence, was truly threatened by lack of food and starvation. When we restrict food, our body has no idea we are doing it intentionally for weight loss, so it actually works to store more fat after the initial weight loss in fear of starvation and death. This protective mechanism is why rapid weight loss from a restrictive diet very rarely yields long term results.

According to Mark Hyman, the average person gains 11 pounds for every diet they go on because of the protective mechanism I previously described.[93] In learning this and watching it play out in the lives of those around me, I often find myself confused as to how faith in dieting is still incredibly common. Yet if I'm being honest, I remember how the vulnerable version of myself who was struggling with an eating disorder would cling to any false hope that a diet would make me skinny and happy. I truly understand what it's like to live in the *diet mentality* and be on what seems like the never ending pursuit of getting skinny dressed up as a way of being "healthy."

Our society's "thin is better" mentality makes the appeal of the promised result so intense that dieting has really become an American past time. In fact, according to Boston Medical, an estimated 45 million Americans are on a diet at any given time each year, yet our health continues to decline.[94] Obviously, diets don't work, so how do we free ourselves from the alluring promise of them and relinquish our need for control by counting calories, tracking macros and weighing ourselves? Let's dive in.

Step 1: Be a Disciple

Stephen Covey, author of the book "7 Habits of Highly Successful People", talks about discipline and its integral role in accomplishing things in our lives. As you know, many chalk up their lack of success with eating a certain way or adopting a healthy lifestyle to a lack of willpower, self-control, and discipline. Having the ability to control our behavior with willpower can only last for so long though. As I mentioned previously, willpower is a very limited resource but we so often resort to it because we have been taught that self-control is all we need to create change in our lives.

Trying to exert control on a facet of our lives that has nothing to do with willpower is not only incredibly stressful, but it is a lost cause. The American Psychological Association does an annual stress survey and year after year participants are asked a variety of questions to assess their interpretation of various aspects of life and how it impacts their mental well-being. Interestingly enough, when participants were asked about their ability to make healthy lifestyle changes, willpower was regularly cited as the number 1 reason for not following through with such changes. Yet according to Covey, following through with making changes has absolutely nothing to do with willpower. Well heck yes!

Putting the biology aside, which almost always wins in the end, our reasons for wanting change are *very* powerful. Covey explains that most people blame their lack of discipline as their main fault in why making any type of change in their lives has not occurred. But the fundamental problem is that "their priorities [to create a healthy lifestyle] have not become deeply planted in their hearts and minds." Thinking that willpower and discipline is what we need is likening change to the mentality that we have to force things *to happen* or force them *not to happen*. Exerting brute force on your life to create change does not sound appealing, and actually goes against what our higher self wants most. I always ask my clients to ask themselves what feels like self-control and what feels like self-care. When we are coming from a place of self-control we are trying to use willpower to make something happen or coming from a place of shameful obligation. When we are coming from a place of self-care, we are taking action aligned with our values and coming from a place of authentic inspiration. When we are truly and deeply connected to what it is that we want most, we are then pulled, *or willed*, into action.

Covey points out that the root word of *discipline* is *disciple*. A disciple is a follower or student to a teacher, leader or philosopher. The key to having discipline is being a disciple to the deep seeded values that make you who you are. What change really comes down to is being aware of what matters most to you, connecting to it and deciding to give a damn about making your ideals a reality.

If you want to change your relationship to food and develop Body Wisdom, I encourage you to spend some time thinking about your "why." What is truly in your heart, deep in your mind, and resonates in your soul?

Having the Perfect Body Does Not Equal the Perfect Life

Surely, it is not just having the perfect body and looking a certain way. What is on the other side of your health and weight loss goal? So many of us think that having the perfect body means having the perfect life or finally being happy. We believe that if *"I could just lose this weight I can be confident, find the perfect partner, get more respect, love, acceptance, connectedness"*, ect. Instead of pursuing what is really important, such as experiencing more joy, love, connection and happiness, we get caught up in the false hope that weight-loss will bring all of those things.

Sadly, this only distracts us from what really matters.

Why do you want to make changes in the first place?

Why is your health so important?

What will be possible for you once this "food and health thing" is all sorted out?

The answers to these questions are where the magic lies and are the essential ingredients in creating the Body Wisdom you've been craving so that you can finally have a meaningful relationship with food and your body. To create change based on our deep-rooted values, we have to want to create a balanced relationship with food more than we want to control and manipulate our body. We have to prioritize our sanity and mental health by rejecting our socially influenced desire to force our bodies to change. We have to release the pressure to have our food look a certain way. We have to accept all of our body instead of being at war with it. We have to understand that what we think will only be available to us "once we lose the weight" is actually already at your fingertips.

You just have to look a little deeper.

When we are passion driven, we become internally ignited with motivation which leads to the fulfillment of our desires and goals that results in increased happiness in our lives. When we are happy and understand how to nourish our bodies, we naturally want to treat ourselves with respect and eat foods that do our body good. I feel it necessary to reiterate that wanting "the perfect body," or "a bikini body" or "to be skinny" does not qualify as a compelling reason "*why*" you want to create change, because your body size does not dictate anything about the value of who you are or how big your life can be. That goal basically means that something is intrinsically not ok about you- that you need to be molded and changed which is probably a pretty painful view to have of yourself. We have to understand that hating ourselves all these years has not gotten the results that we have wanted, so it's time to try loving ourselves as we are instead.

Accept your body and accept your life. We can do both and still want to make changes that align with what's truly important to us. We can spend more time creating the life we want as oppose to fixing what we think is wrong with it.

Focusing on the way we look is confining, and limits our self-expression. But that doesn't mean you can't care about your appearance. We all want to look and feel beautiful, but focusing solely on the way we look or the size of our body is a recipe for disordered eating, body image issues, and a decreased sense of self-worth. When we give away our power to the way we look, we end up letting it dictate how we are going to act and how we feel about ourselves which almost always leads to more crazy confusion with food and the desire to control. This is why choosing to love, or at least accept, our appearance as it is right now is extremely helpful and necessary in your pursuit of Body Wisdom and food freedom. Body Acceptance allows us to become neutral to our appearance. So instead of living in reaction mode based on how we look, we are able to be in creation mode- choosing how to live our life each day regardless of how we look.

I may sound like a broken record, but I can't put enough emphasis on the concept that the pressure you feel to change your body starts from the external world. External oppression and arbitrary societal constructs of beauty, is what started the distrust of your body in the first place. Not only are we in many ways intentionally confused about the nutrition of food and food-like products, we are culturally taught to instill value in our outward appearance, but it pales in comparison to the value that your uniqueness can offer the world.

It is flat out wrong to say that health and happiness looks like a specific body size, so I encourage you to reject that idea entirely and give a big

"F-you" to diet culture. Stand up for yourself and choose to support body diversity, body positivity, and body acceptance. Accepting yourself the way you are is necessary if you want to develop Body Wisdom. You will not turn into an un-loveable pig if you love and accept yourself, you do not have to be a size 4 to be worthy of your own love, and your opinion of your body has nothing to do with the opinions others have. I'd actually be willing to bet that loving yourself and choosing to be confident will make you a more pleasant person to be around. Plus, your health will fare better if you loved yourself more, since we know (scientifically and intuitively) that there truly is a mind-body connection at work. It isn't farfetched to assume that loving yourself will improve your health and your enjoyment in life, regardless of any changes in weight or appearance.

Creating Your Healthy Vision For Life

Now that you know you have permission to love yourself exactly as you are, what is your optimal vision for your health and your life? Don't be shy here, go all out! Really put your heart on the line. What is it that you truly want? What does it feel like? What types of thoughts will you be having?

Often times, we are so busy with the day to day tasks of life that we don't slow down enough to let ourselves really dream and ponder these very important questions because we are so caught up in the pursuit of having the perfect body, and finding the perfect way to eat. We numb and distract ourselves by staring into our cell phones, deep in a scroll hole of social media feeds, absorbing messages from the outside world that add pressure to that pursuit and often disconnects us more from our body.

What is on the other side of body dissatisfaction?

What is it that you tell yourself you can't have until you are satisfied with your body?

Allow yourself, rather *give* yourself the time and the space to turn inward and really sit with this. And don't hold back, no matter how far-fetched and impossible it seems, remember that humans have been to outer space, we have handheld super computers as cell phones, and we are living in a time when self-driving cars are becoming a reality. Heck we are even growing organs for transplants which is creepy and cool at the same time. So hopefully those outrageous realties open you up to possibility for your own life. And trust me I have a point with all of this so bear with me until the end.

Once you have the vision and goal of what could be possible once you start loving yourself and living fully self-expressed, start to break down the various components of how to accomplish this vision into small digestible parts. To make it easier to visualize and figure out what needs to happen, look at your vision as *macro* and *micro goals*.

Let's say, you might want to reverse an autoimmune disease or recover from an eating disorder, which would be considered a *macro goal*. In order to accomplish those larger visions, we have to understand what we need to do daily to get there. This vision will not happen overnight and will be the accumulation of effort, practice and action each day over a period of time. The daily actions you take to accomplish your macro goal are the *micro goals,* and you can think of these as stepping stones along the road to your transformation, vision and/or goal.

To figure out what those micro actions are, it's helpful to think in reverse and work backwards from the end goal to create the road map from where you are now to where you want to be. This is a huge part of what I do with my health coaching clients. We might have a clear image of where we want to be and how we want to feel each day, but perhaps the steps required to reach the destination are less obvious. If I am working with a client who is not exactly sure how to get to their ideal endpoint, I help design the road map (aka micro daily/weekly goals) to get them there. It's the little actions we take each day that add up to massive change in our body and in our lives. And we cannot change our lives unless we change what we do daily.

Although we have previously touched on the topic of mindset, establishing a mental outlook that is rooted in self-love and self-care will continue to play an integral role in aligning your daily actions with your long term goal. Knowing that we are worthy of a better life and capable of daily self-love will help us stay aligned with the necessary actions that coincide with our micro and macro goals. Believe it or not, your body can hear every thought you have. Positive and negative affirmations truly do impact our body on a deep, physiological levels that often goes unnoticed by the conscious mind. It is important that you start to bring awareness to how you speak to yourself right now. If you often default to demeaning and self-deprecating thoughts when you make a mistake, look in the mirror, or post a picture to Instagram, it is time to turn up the self-love and instead choose a few empowering affirmations that feel good to you, and only you.

This stuff really matters, and it's ok to have an off day here and there, that's life and its ok to be down about it, you have every right to feel your feelings, just keep coming back to your empowering self-affirmations. Learning to course correct automatically without it needing to be a huge and dramatic "re-inventing yourself" event, will help you flow seamlessly between self-love being your default and using affirmations as a reset button when things go awry.

Just brush yourself off and get back to it. It doesn't need to be some grand event, New Year's resolution or a total revamp of your life starting Monday. It can be moment to moment. You really are worth it, as cliché and annoying as that may sound!

The more you learn to automatically course correct, the easier it gets, and you will find your days being overwhelmed with peace and joy instead of anxiety and frustration. Learning to autocorrect with ease brings me to my next point in creating effective and lasting change through Body Wisdom:

Consistency

When we make the decision that we are finally ready to make changes in our lives, we have to be consistent in those micro actions in order to accomplish our macro goals. If your macro goal is to recover from an eating disorder, heal from IBS, break free from the diet game, or any other self-love or self-care motivated endpoint, consistency is absolutely essential. No matter your age, gender, race, socioeconomic status, or profession, creating long-term change boils down to how consistent you are with the daily actions that will deliver the results you want.

To achieve long term results, we need a long term solution which is where consistency comes into play. Simon Sinek, a motivational speaker and author explains "that we cannot go to the gym, workout for 9 hours and get in shape. It doesn't matter how hard you push yourself or how many calories you burn it just won't happen. But if you work out for 20 minutes every day you will absolutely get in shape, *over time*." The dilemma that we as a culture of instant gratification grapple with is knowing when the result will be achieved. Predicting a timeline for our macro goals is a hard metric to nail down, but we do know beyond certainty that taking small actions everyday (such as exercising for 20 minutes every day) will drastically improve your health *with time*.[95] Simon explains that intensity, (aka dieting, 30 day slim downs, cleanses etc.), is like going to the dentist. "[the appointment is] fixed in time, we know exactly what date we're going, we know how long we're going to be there and we know that when we come out our teeth will feel smooth and look pearly, but if that's all we do, all our teeth will fall out. In other words, intensity is not enough."

He continues, "we also have to brush our teeth twice a day every day for two minutes. While the impact of those two minutes on their own is hard to identify we know that doing it every day will keep our gums and teeth healthy."

"But for how long do we have to keep up this daily habit before we see changes?" And how many days of brushing could we skip before we see a decline in oral hygiene?

The hard truth is that we don't really know. It's a harder metric to measure which is why we like intensity rather than consistency. We like things that are fixed and measurable with a predetermined result announced up front. We like to know when we are going to see results. That is why we like intense measures such as dieting, 30-day slim downs and juice cleanses or temporary changes.

To bring this analogy back to our health and Body Wisdom, we can't expect that eating perfectly for 30 days will provide us with results that will last for the rest of our life. We have to do the food-based equivalent of brushing our teeth twice a day, every day. We have to eat SOUL-food (sprinkled in with some of our favorite comfort foods of course) that makes us feel good, consistently, over the course of time in order to achieve the results we desire.

Although I do not know exactly how long you'll have to eat *SOUL-fully*, practice self-love and work on your micro daily actions before you will begin to see results, I do know that eventually your life and relationship to food will change for the better. While that is simple to understand in theory, it is more challenging to execute. Choosing to approach change through the mindset of intensity by dramatically changing the way you eat and live all at once is incredibly stressful, and very difficult to maintain in the long run. It's why trying to "eat perfectly" by way of willpower often results in rebound binges. This is why I continue to advocate that you choose *consistency* over *intensity* by incorporating small acts, or micro goals, over time that add up to create lifelong shifts. No matter the good intentions that motivate a short period of intensity, small positive actions fulfilled with consistency will always produce greater long term results.

Eating a salad one day at lunch is fantastic. Going on a walk after dinner, bravo! Repeating positive affirmations in the mirror when stressed, you go Glen Coco! [96] Doing just one of these acts on their own or for a short period of time does absolutely nothing for overall health, but the accumulation of those small acts consistently over the course of day, months and years, absolutely will.

One day you will wake up and have changed your habits, love your body, be in-tune with it, no longer feel so crazy around food, potentially be off your medication and walking upstairs without getting winded.

I just can't tell you when.

3 months, 6 months, a year? I do not know how long you will have to do those small consistent acts before you see the results you want.

But I know beyond certainty that one day you will. If you want to come to a healthy weight for your body, change the trajectory of your health, recover from your eating disorder, or heal digestive issues, you have to do small things every. single. day.

You have to be consistent, not intense.

To review, here are the three distinctions that dwarf the need for willpower in your pursuit of lasting lifestyle change:
1. A powerful, emotionally moving reason "why." i.e. being the disciple of change.
2. Clear vision and goals, then breaking the large vision into small digestible little nuggets
3. Consistency, also known as repetition and practice. Slow, steady sustainable change.

Chapter 11 ACTION STEPS:

Discovery #1: What truly matters to you in your life? What type of freedom, acceptance, self-expression, purpose, or change for yourself and the world would you like to see or be a part of?

Discovery #2: What are your Macro Visions or Goals? Why are these goals so important to you? What would be possible if you brought them to life?

Discovery #3: What are two to three Micro actions you could start doing consistently, every day that will, over time, change your life and help bring you closer to your macro vision? Pick one. Start there. Commit to it, and do it every damn day.

12

EATING WELL IS AN ACT OF REBELLION

"We don't need to solve our problems, we only need to put our attention on problems bigger than ourselves. The antidote to self-consciousness is not self-improvement, but other-consciousness."

—Brandilyn Tebo

As humans, we are naturally inclined to be really concerned with ourselves, it's the ego in all of us. We put pressure on ourselves to look a certain way, say the right thing, do the right thing and often take actions from a self-conscious space in a constant fear of judgement from others. Not only is this almost always painful, but we rarely get the results that we want and we often feel dis-empowered in the process. Even if we do succeed, the feelings of joy will be temporary if we operate from a place of seeking approval.

As important as it is to take care of ourselves, love ourselves and understand what we want from our Body Wisdom, shifting attention outside of ourselves can sometimes be the necessary catalyst for the changes that we really want to make. This was my experience while in recovery from my eating disorder and in pursuit of my Body Wisdom. Once I realized there was a much larger problem then the size of my body, I was now free to focus my attention on that which released my desire to be in control, relinquished my fear of weight gain and inspired

me to eat foods that made me feel good; simply because there was now
so much more at stake. This chapter explains the problem I set out to
improve. My experience may or may not inspire action in you but it was
very important to my own journey and it serves as a positive example of
how to release the ego driven need for control and make my meals mean
something more significant to the world at large.

In a world where we are taught that...

▶   health comes in one size

▶   beauty looks one way

▶   industry profits are more important than public health

▶   the environment is ours to destroy

▶   animal welfare has little value

▶   human rights are subjective,

...then actively choosing to eat nourishing SOUL foods becomes an *act
of rebellion*. It becomes something way bigger than just our own body and
health.

**In essence by choosing SOUL-food and connecting to our
Body Wisdom we are standing up against:**

▶   large food companies and their processed and packaged products

▶   9 out of 10 aisles in the average grocery store

▶   cultural conditioning

▶   hormone-disrupting and disease causing food-like stuff that is
    artificially cheap because of government subsidizes and back
    door dealings

▶   corruption from insurance agencies and pharmaceutical
    companies

▶   exploitation of natural resources and our environment

▶   mistreatment of animals and agricultural workers and farmers

▶   lobbyist with corporate interest in mind

▶   direct to consumer advertising that is misleading and manipulative

- ▸ advertising to children who are easily influenced to eat heavily processed and sugar-laden foods
- ▸ deceptive sales practices of products that contribute to chronic disease
- ▸ unrealistic beauty standards, the myths of a general healthy weight and perceived value of an arbitrary body size

As much as I care about individual health and Body Wisdom, once the issue became bigger than me, the way I fed myself morphed into a form of activism and a representation of the world I wanted to live in. Once I had a bigger problem than my own pursuit of body perfection, I felt so much more free around food.

Admittingly, this chapter almost didn't make it into the book. Diving into the topic of eating as an act of rebellion felt like potentially opening up a can of worms. Yet I realized that I couldn't write an entire book on what helped me make peace with food and helped me develop my Body Wisdom if I didn't have a chapter on the greater problems in the world that allowed me to redirect my ego-centric focus towards that of the greater good.

I no longer had to look at eating SOUL-fully as a punishment or as a way to manipulate my body size or to prove my self-worth. I no longer felt the urge to eat healthfully because I "should" or it was the "right" food. I wanted to eat whole foods not only so that I felt better physically, but because I knew it was having a greater impact on the world around me.

I stopped obsessing and feeling crazy around food when I became aware of the implications of animal agriculture on the environment, commodity crops on food prices, and the corruption of our food industry that puts profits before the welfare of the people who are consuming the heavily processed and artificial-ingredient laden "food-like" products that do not provide real nourishment and our body does not truly recognize. Often these low quality foods are what people have access to because of socio-economic injustices. Once I became aware of the politics in food, I became my own version of an activist.

Rewind time to when I entered into my recovery phase from my eating disorder, and this is right around the time I started to self-educate about our food industry. I picked up a book for the first time in a few years and put down my fashion magazines. Then documentaries like Food Inc., Forks Over Knives and Food Matters had become available on Netflix. The information within these documentaries started me on the path of shifting my understanding of food, which really helped to transform my relationship with it. Eating was no longer just about me and my body size, it was about standing up for what I believed in and this made me feel empowered to make more healthful choices without stress, guilt or shame.

I really feel like this chapter is a doozy. So here goes nothing.

Plant Based Diets and Veganism

The concept of Veganism dates back to the 1940s, but it was a wildly new idea to me in my early twenties when I stumbled across the book *Skinny Bitch* by Rory Freedman and Kim Barnouin. The cover and title drew me in because of its provocative nature, but it presented some radically new ideas to me in a very tart-tongue and cheeky way. As a girl with an affinity for profanity, I laughed my entire way through that book and very seriously considered transitioning to a plant based diet on the spot. Albeit well intentioned, this book did prey and profit upon women's desire to be thin, which in hindsight I don't love (*at all*), but it left an impression on me and I became resolutely curious to learn more about plant based diets. Never before in my life had someone argued against the consumption of meat, let alone in a conspicuously hilarious way. Up until that point, I had only been preached to about the importance of a high animal protein, low carb diet for "health" and of course for weight-loss.

Upon googling for more books on plant based diets, I came across *The China Study* by T. Colin Campbell. For those unfamiliar, it combines years of nutritional research from Campbell's team at Cornell in conjunction with teams in both China and England to conduct a study on diet and the implications for chronic diseases. To give you the abridged version, it concludes that a whole foods, plant based diet is the among the healthiest on the planet for longevity and an increase in animal consumption is undoubtedly linked to chronic disease (This isn't to say that all animal consumption is, rather quality, quantity and source all play a role). Learning about the connection between food and health outside of the world of weight-loss was transformative to say the least. While I had always just said I wanted to be healthy (when really the goal was to be skinny), this absolutely shifted something inside of me. Without even a blink of my eye, learning about the relationship between food, health, environment, politics, animals and society at large was hugely influential on my journey to where I am now— a SOUL food servin' Health Coach with my own unique sense of Body Wisdom.

Dirty Agriculture: Farm Bills, Subsidies, and Seed Saving

In the midst of this all, I almost became a bit radicalized in my pursuit of veganism but it might not be for the reasons you are thinking. About halfway through reading the China Study I watched Food Inc. and for a lack of a better word I became *enraged*. Like any person who feels like they have been lied to and manipulated, I was flat out pissed about the corruption taking place in our food industry. I learned about the mistreatment of small farmers by large corporations like Monsanto. How they would no longer allow farmers to save seeds and would sue independent farms if their organic farms had become polluted with Monsanto's patented GMO seed because of no fault but the wind. I learned about the revolving door of employees between large corporations and the government agencies that regulated their industries. It became clear that there was abuse and unethical behavior happening at the highest levels of our government in conjunction with big business that was (and still is) negatively affecting the food supply, animals, people's health, and the planet. I started to learn why Twinkies with about 35 ingredients cost less than a bunch of beets. Immediately, eating was no longer about me but rather about something much bigger and completely outside of myself.

I continued to research and dig in to the corrupt and greedy practices of our food industry. I learned that in the United States, we have what are called *Farm Bills*. Although this term has the word *"farm"* in it, they are not really about *farming* as much as they are about *producing* food. At face value, farming and producing food may sound similar, but with the processes of modern agriculture farming and producing food are in fact, two totally different industries that impart two very different effects on food availability, cost, and marketing. Have you ever wondered why the majority of our supermarkets are 90% full of processed foods? What about the reasoning behind why the most expensive items are often whole fruits, vegetables, whole grains, nuts, seeds and organic pasture raised meat and eggs? Look no further than the Farm Bills.

Farm Bills are complicated, lengthy and unglamorous pieces of legislation that basically decide what the rules of the American food system are by determining what crops will get government subsidies. This is why the completely processed, man-made cake-like thing that is a Twinkie is cheaper than mama earths simple roots. These bills also favor the production of genetically modified corn, soy, wheat, cotton and rice, but predominantly corn and soy. As the American population has increased in size and decreased in health, U.S. agriculture has been shilling out support upwards of *$25 billion dollars* a year in taxpayer money towards the crops that produce the foods that make us sick and leave behind almost everything else that is of nutritional value.[97] An example from the book *Health at Every Size*, by Linda Bacon explains a raw potato might cost .50 cents a pound but once transformed into potato chips, they sell for about $4 a pound.[98] It's described in marketing terms as "added value" when really it's just adding on profit for big agribusiness. It is not sheer coincidence that the $4/pound potato chip tastes better and is more desirable than its former version of the humble spud. Rather it is the work of clever scientists who have been hired by the food industry giants to manipulate the ingredients of processed food to make the taste irresistible while doing absolutely nothing to actually satisfy hunger or meet nutritional needs. These foods are the most sophisticated foods on the planet, designed to taste amazing but do little to activate our hormonal responses or turn on our body's weight regulation system. This means we can eat a lot of these foods and not actually feel full.

Processed foods provide large profits because the raw materials, such as the .50 cent/pound potato, are cheap. Furthermore, Dr. Linda Bacon, explains that "a bushel of corn has more than 130,000 food calories. Enough, in theory, to feed a person for over two months. A bushel of corn costs only about $4. That means that a full years-worth of corn calories costs less than $25, and the reason is it so cheap is because of another dirty aspect of our food industry known as *government subsidies*.

Our food system and modern agriculture is one of the few industries that does not run like most: on the free market of supply and demand which leads to natural price increase and decrease. Typically, if supply is high and demand is low then prices are low and suppliers slow production. Not in agriculture. The opposite is true because the government pays the farmers for specific crops even if they cannot sell them. It literally incentivizes farmers to over produce regardless if there is a demand because the government will pay them no matter what. Let's say that a bushel of corn costs $1 to produce and the market value is only .75 cents, the government will pay the farmer the missing .25 cents and a little extra for profit. Its estimated that 50% of grain farmers net income comes from these government subsidies, AKA your tax dollars.[98] Gosh if that doesn't piss you the fuck off, then keep reading to learn how this surplus of cheap grain has impacted other areas of our world. It might not surprise you to learn that these bills do little to support or encourage farmers to grow other fresh fruits and vegetables. The way in which our government financially supports the prioritization of cheap grains is why the most unhealthful food is almost always the cheapest. *Dirt cheap* grains that are then turned into *even cheaper* processed "food-like" products, artificially drive up the cost of production of SOUL-food. Our "free-market" has become so heavily skewed by the overwhelming amount of cheap processed foods that affording quality foods like organic fruits and vegetables are reserved for those with a higher income status. This disproportionate access to healthful food has become so prevalent now, that the biggest predictor of obesity is income level.

Although the meat and dairy industry are not the *direct* recipients of these agricultural subsidiaries, these industries benefit massively from the dirt cheap production of grain, corn, and soy because much of the surplus crops are fed to cows, chicken and pigs, which drives down the cost of meat production. The overproduction of cheap GMO corn and soy is why we have switched to providing feedlot animals with grains for their primary food, when they are biologically designed to eat primarily grass. Toss aside the fact that consuming grain makes these animals sick, which therefore increases their need for pharmaceuticals, but it also lowers the nutritional value of the meat. Simply put, we are not eating the same high quality food previous generations did, we are getting meat from sick animals, and a surplus of processed foods all at the expense of our health, environment and natural resources while we line the pockets of a few big businesses.

Furthermore, as the world's appetite for meat has increased we have started to feed most of the grain we grow to cows and not people. Since

10 pounds of grain produces 1 pound of beef, many more people are bound to go to without food.[99] If we pulled back on our production of industrialized animals we could arguably feed the people of the world. But there are many industries invested in the production of industrially raised animals.

The amount of pharmaceuticals used on livestock such as antibiotics to keep animals healthy from a lack of their natural diet, hormones to keep female cows producing milk, and growth hormones to increase the feed efficiency of animals has made the meat industry the largest customer of the most powerful drug companies in the world.[100] To top it all off, GMO crops that have been genetically designed to resist herbicides and pesticides are sprayed with Monsanto's RoundUp that contains glyphosate and is the most widely used herbicide in the world. [101] The World Health Organization classified glyphosate as "probably carcinogenic to humans," and can cause mutations in DNA. Almost all conventional crops in this country are sprayed with RoundUp and then those plants, be it corn, soy or wheat, are fed to the animals that are slaughtered for consumption or are sold to companies who turn the that polluted grain into cheap *food-like* stuff for humans.

These companies certainly do not want their business to dwindle and are in thick with lobbyists to ensure our lawmakers act in their best interest. In fact, by law companies are required to act in the best interest of their *shareholders*, not in public health, animal welfare or environmental sustainability. Even if someone of substantial power and influence within these companies actually had a moral compass and wanted to conduct business in an ethical fashion that considered the health of consumers and the planet, they can only do so if it will make them money. Companies are legally bound to do what will make their shareholders more money so if a change decreases profits they can be held liable for damages and be sued. Our system is literally set up to benefit big business, and neglect the health of consumers, animals and our planet.

Learning about this made me realize how meaningful choosing SOUL-foods could actually be. When we look beyond personal health, a thin body, or any other individualized goal, eating well becomes a political and moral issue that affects the entire world around us. Let alone feeling better, and having more energy to be the person I wanted to be, nourishing my body was voting with my wallet against this corporate greed and government corruption that pisses off every cell in my body. I did not want to be complicit in this shit.

Even the United States food pyramid and food plate are designed by the US Department of Agriculture, that absolutely places its interest in support of agribusiness over consumer health. Do not be confused, the recommendations from our government on what the building blocks of a healthful diet are, are overwhelmingly influenced by the interests of big business. The federal government will purchase surplus food (dairy, meat, eggs, corn, soy) for distribution in public schools through the National School Lunch Program and food assistance programs like WIC (Women Infants and Children). Go into any public school or observe what foods are available for purchase with food assistance coupons and you will notice that the majority of these foods are processed, packaged, and lacking in nutritional value. Why? Simply because our current crop subsidies have made fresh fruits and vegetables substantially more expensive and difficult for assistance programs and public schools to afford. This means that low quality and nutritionally void food surpluses of corn, soy, and wheat are the foods that are being fed to our country's most vulnerable populations: women, children, and lower income families. Just writing this chapter gives me goosebumps as I think about how powerful our food choices really are and how much deeper they go than our own desire for personal health or getting thinner.

Conventional meat, dairy, chicken, eggs, processed and fast foods are artificially cheap because it is convoluted with hidden costs far greater than what we see at the supermarket checkout. Conventional animal agriculture is the largest contributor to climate change, air and ground water pollution, and deforestation around the world.[102] If you at all care about the planet, it's hard to ignore what is on your plate. While I am not advocating for a vegan diet, I am adamantly arguing for more SOUL-food and that includes whole fruits and vegetables, nuts, seeds and organic, grass fed, pasture raised animal products.

I did spend 7 years on a plant based diet and it helped me heal from my eating disorder simply because eating wasn't about my body but instead about the world. During this time, I did not know that grass-fed and pasture raised animal products were necessarily an option and they certainly weren't within my price range. Eating vegan is what made the most sense and I was inspired by the ripple effect of a more conscious and compassionate way of eating could have.

While transitioning into a plant based diet was hugely influential to my overall health, I have learned through my education and furthering my knowledge in nutrition that there is not a "one-size fits all" perfect diet. Although I felt passionately about veganism for a very long time, I have learned to honor the individuality of each person and advocate for a SOUL-full diet that brings awareness to the power of choice within our food market. The purpose of this chapter is to not preach veganism, but rather to shed light on why choosing SOUL-food encompasses so much more than just individualized health and body size.

Having been so strong in my conviction to eat and live a certain way only to later change my mind upon more education has made me a more compassionate and tolerant person. Seeing how I could shift my perspective and how my point of view could change has made me more understanding of others and how they choose to live their lives. After years on a strictly plant-based diet I could tell my body was telling me I needed animal protein, so I added back in eggs and I felt better instantly. It's experiences like that of my own that have helped form my opinions on individual health that I have now.

With that being said, the ethical reasons for why NOT to eat meat are really obvious to me. Animals are often raised and killed in unbearable and cruel conditions. Grain that could feed all the hungry people in this country is instead fed to cows that are biologically designed to eat grass, and get sick on a diet of grains. Massive amounts of land and water is needed to raise animal livestock in CAFOS or *Concentrated Animal Feed Operations,* and this excessive utilization of natural resources promotes deforestation and uses up our water supply irresponsibly. Most antibiotics and prescription drugs are given to factory farmed animals which we then consume. In addition, eating meat ultimately means killing a sentient being.[103] Aside from the last side-effect of industrial animal livestock that I listed, all the other aspects are conditional and dependent on how the animal is raised. This ability to transform the impact of conventionally raised livestock on our world is why you will see a huge societal push for organic and pasture-raised animal products. This cultural shift is part of the reason why I have slowly changed my perspective on eating animals based on these specific conditions.

Very few people would argue that the current way in which most meat and poultry is produced is not ecologically harmful and ethically wrong. However, there are examples of how livestock can be beneficial for sustainable agriculture and be a part of the circle of life. For example, cows convert energy from the sun into food more efficiently then we can without the use of fossil fuels. Cows eat the grass, use its energy to grow big and strong, break down the nutrients and poop to fertilize the land. The sun then shines upon the fertilized land and through photosynthesis, the grass grows again for the cows to eat and the cycle continues. This symbiotic relationship is summed up well in Aldo Leopold's concept of land ethics: "a thing is right when it tends to preserve the integrity, stability and beauty of the biotic community. It is wrong when it tends otherwise." Eating small amounts of locally sourced, grass-fed beef, pigs and pastured chickens is in many ways honoring the cycle of life.

It is the modern manipulation of this process and overconsumption of conventionally raised animals that has contributed to the grotesque treatment of animals, misuse of natural resources, corrupt backdoor dealings, and the irresponsible polluting of our environment.

The corrupt nature of the conventional livestock industry is hugely influential in my overall desire for people to eat more plants. However, plants are not completely exempt from this excessive consumption of natural resources, greed, and there are some plants that are produced in a way that is harmful for the planet as well. A pastured animal is beneficial to the environment and in some ways more ethical then the fossil fueled reality of tractor fields for irrigated soy, corn, canola and cotton that requires a lot processing. These crops are heavily sprayed with herbicides and pesticides and then used to make some of the most unhealthy foods, many of which are in fact vegan.

Oreos, Frittos, unfrosted Pop Tarts, Sour Patch Kids, Earth Balance vegan butter, Duncan Hines Creamy Homestyle Frosting and many more are vegan and are made from the processing of industrialized farming crops. Most of these are clever renditions of commodity crops and are loaded with High Fructose Corn Syrup or processed vegetable oils that are a product of this heavily processed and industrialized system. These crops and their products contribute to the social economic and health divide we see amongst Americans of various income levels. Conventional animal agriculture and commodity crops are both wildly abusive of our resources and destructive to the health of consumers, which is why choosing SOUL-food for me is an emotionally moving vote I can make with my hard-earned dollars- not just eating vegan (or gluten free and soy free) products.

Don't get me wrong, I will eat an Oreo from time to time and enjoy it, but learning about what goes on behind the scenes of the supermarket shelf made me a conscious consumer. It transformed the way I ate into a politically motivated issue, which left no room for my concern with being a specific body size. Unfortunately, the corruption involved in making processed foods cheaper than fruits and vegetables extends beyond the supermarket. As I mentioned previously, our large non-profit organizations have a list of corporate sponsors that influence the recommendations they provide. Many of which are in opposition to logical thinking.

Corporate Sponsorship and Systemic Greed

Similar to the coconut oil scandal that involved the American Heart Association and the Canola Oil industry in 2017 that I mentioned in the beginning of this book, in 2003 The American Academy of Pediatric Dentistry accepted $1 million in funding from Coca-Cola. It would seem strange that an organization dedicated to dental health would accept money from a corporation devoted to producing sugary, cavity-producing soft drinks, right? When confronted about the controversial funding, they AAPD provided the defense that there is "little scientific evidence that soft drinks play a role in children's oral disease." [104] Even our most prominent nutrition organizations that are designed to provide reliable recommendations for the general public have been co-opted by corporate companies. The American Dietetic Association (ADA) has corporate sponsors that pay for the rights to write the ADA fact sheets for the nutritional recommendations for our country. These companies include The National Soft Drink Association, McDonalds, The Steel Packaging Council and Mars (the candy company). No offense, but these are companies that are involved in creating cheap and heavily processed food-like products that contribute to the already suffering health of our country. Allowing companies such as these (whose sole mission is to turn a profit by selling SAD foods) have no place in the role of creating the nutritional guidelines for our country. As Linda Bacon has explained before, unfortunately Co-Opting professionals is just business as usual in this country and a widely used corporate strategy to increase profit.

Even the education for medical professionals including physicians and dieticians comes from Nutrition in Medicine and the Medical Nutrition Curriculum Initiative.[105] These organizations are supported by the Egg Nutrition Board, The Dannon Institute, National Cattlemen's Beef Institute, National Dairy Council, Nestle Clinical Nutrition, Wyeth-Ayerst Laboratories and Baxter Healthcare Corporation. That means the expensive education received by our leading health professionals is undoubtedly biased towards supporting the over consumption of conventional animal products and the over prescribing of pharmaceuticals. No wonder the healing nature of plant foods are not given their fair share of attention at the higher education level for our medical professionals — it would affect the bottom line (profit) of corporate sponsors.

Other Consciousness as a Solution

I care about this planet and I want to be healthy. So transitioning to a predominantly organic, whole foods, plant rich diet made sense to me. It inspired change in me because I now had *other*-consciousness to put my attention on. I was no longer *self*-conscious and focusing my energy on trying to fix all my problems with food, control what I ate, or feel sorry for myself because I didn't have the perfect body. I was inspired to eat in a way that made me feel good physically, mentally, emotionally, and in a way that made a difference on a larger scale. The ripple effect was what I was after. This is also why I began to strive to eat organic as much as possible and started to advocate for sustainable agriculture. There are downstream implications felt in all facets of our society when we ignore the health, moral, and ethical implications of our food system, and I wasn't willing to be complacent to these repercussions.

As Tony Robbins has said "it's not about being more strong willed, its' about being more fulfilled." I became more fulfilled by eating this way because it empowered me to be the change I wanted to see in the world. Like with the Stephen Covey's example, I became a disciple to my deep-seeded values of creating a more fair and just world where the health of our people and planet matter more than profit.

This is why I truly believe that choosing SOUL-food, eating well, and nourishing your body is an act of rebellion against a corrupt system that neglects your health and well-being. It's amazing to me how part of healing my relationship with food, was having it no longer be just about me.

Chapter 12 ACTION STEPS:

Discovery #1: What is a possible reason outside of yourself that you can think of for eating a more SOUL-food lifestyle? How could this reason help you develop Body Wisdom?

Discovery #2: What is an *other*-consciousness that has potential to be the antidote to your *self*-consciousness?

13

BECOMING YOUR OWN HEALTH EXPERT

"The only rule is there are NO rules."

—Cara (yeah, that's me and I am quoting myself! Sue me.)

B y now you know a little bit more about my personal journey
and how I came to develop Body Wisdom. It was a process and
a practice that took time. While it was deeply rooted in self-love, self-care,
and holistic nutrition, it was also heavily influenced by my interpretation
of the world around me. But here comes the fun part: It's now time to
explore how you can bring everything together that you just learned in
the previous chapters to create and develop your own Body Wisdom.

Redefine Health for Yourself

One of the most important elements in developing Body Wisdom
is to decide what health means for you. As I've touched on before, there
are millions of people telling you what you should be doing and how you
should be living your life. Just like there is abundant information available
about what is healthy and what is not. Arguably, this book is just one
more person telling you one more piece of information in that realm.

While my intention is to help you connect more to your own body,
I did that by sharing a personal perspective on what health means for me

and the information I believe to be true. That doesn't mean it is true or right for you- only you can decide that for yourself.

Step one in developing Body Wisdom is to make up your own definition for what optimal health means to you. You do not have to accept everything you are told at face value as hard truths for you and your life. You have permission to interpret everything on your own accord and take it or leave it. The beauty of being a unique individual is that you can decide for yourself how you want to create health, nourishment and high vibes.

To give you an example of how two people can live healthy lives that look different, take Lee Tilghman, from Lee From America. She is a holistic health blogger whom I admire and respect immensely. That said, I have zero interest in being alcohol free like she is and I do not make myself wrong for enjoying alcohol nor think I am less healthy. So although her personal definition of health excludes alcohol, for me, my personal definition of health includes alcohol. Health is not just physical and biological, it's also mental, emotional and spiritual, and for me, part of my healthy lifestyle is not denying myself the pleasure and joy I get from having a glass of organic wine or a pint of craft beer.

So what does health mean for you?

Does it mean honoring your body, waking up with energy, vitality, and creativity each day? Does it mean having open and honest conversations with others and living a fully self-expressed life? Does it include cake and kale? Does it mean being confident in your skin regardless of what society tells you? Does it mean working out 4 days a week or whenever the desire strikes? Does it mean being inspired to shop at farmers markets, and cook food for yourself at home? Are you cooking all the time, some of the time, or whenever you have the time?

We put so much pressure on ourselves to live our life a certain way and sometimes I don't think we slow down to even ask ourselves if we WANT to live our life that way. As Cloe Ward so wisely said, "try

to remember not to care about the things you don't even care about."
So what do you actually really care about? What will truly make you
feel good? What is your own definition of health? Ask yourself these
questions and spend time discovering and reflecting on the answers.

Listen to Your Body

Part of defining health for yourself is listening to your own body.
Throughout this book, I have reiterated that there is so much conflicting
information out in the world of health and nutrition leaving many of us
confused. And that the only way to know what is true for you is to slow
down and listen to the information your body sends you. We have to
believe that the answers already lie within.

Furthermore, the way of eating that makes me feel most vibrant and
nourished is probably not the same for you. The truth is, there is no one
right way to eat. The "right" way to eat is the way that makes you feel
good in your body, that's it. It's truly individual and can change from day
to day. It may not be 3 meals a day or 6 meals or intermittent fasting. It
may not be Bulletproof, Keto or low carb. It might not even be slow carb
or high carb either. It may not be vegetarian, vegan, Whole Foods Plant-
Based and here is the real kicker- *it's possibly not SOUL-food either.* The only
way is the way that makes you feel most alive- and that may or may not
look like the way that makes me feel most alive.

One of my all-time favorite bloggers is Emily Schuman from
Cupcakes and Cashmere and I have been following along with her since
2008. While I love almost everything she shares because you can feel
her authentic love and passion, the amount of pastries, candies, cheese
and ice cream she eats would not work for me and my body. For me
personally, it doesn't align with my own definition of health or values
and as you have learned, my body does not feel best when I eat those
foods so I don't have the desire to. Simple as that. This doesn't mean that

she is wrong for eating the way she eats nor does it mean I am right for eating the way I eat. I am listening to my body and she is listening to hers. And I encourage and invite you to listen to yours.

Get curious about the physical sensations and energy moving through your body. When you are constipated, bloated, fatigued, irritable, stressed, nervous, or anxious, slow down and get present. What are these sensations indicative of and what is the message your body is trying to convey. Sometimes slowing down to become a neutral observer and receiver of the sensations going on in our body is challenging. Not only are we often moving a million miles a minute, but we are quick to react to uncomfortable sensations with negativity. Often all we need to do is relax, take a couple deep breathes and instead of wishing the discomfort wasn't there, accept it with compassion and get curious to the meaning of the messages.

Trust Your Body

Often, we look to the outside world to tell us how to eat. We will spend so much time looking for the right diet or perfect way of eating in hopes that it will heal our relationship with food and yield health. This only distracts us from what our body is saying and its putting more faith in external factors than the woven in wisdom.

To become your own health expert you have to trust that your body already has the perfect plan for health programmed into it. As Ingrid Nilsen said on her podcast Ladies Who Lunch, that I was a guest on, "your body is this ultimate truth teller." But if you aren't listening to it, then it isn't doing you any good. Are you ready and willing to trust the sensations and information that it sends to you and invest time in decoding it? The thing about the signals coming from our body is that it is non-biased, neutral information. Its not trying to sell you anything, or tell you what you want to hear, its simply looking out for you and only you; so by default, it really is the most trustworthy source for what will set you up for ultimate vibrancy and aliveness!

Stand Up For Your Body

We live in a world where societal constructs are created and reflective of our political, social and economic environments at any given time. Sadly, many of us let them rule our lives and often we didn't have a choice otherwise. If we look at the history of the United States, we used to have a societal construct where people of color were slaves and counted for 3/5 a vote, known as the 3/5 compromise. [105] Women were not seen as equal so they were not allowed to work outside the home or get an education. We didn't even get the right to vote until 1920. [106] Marriage was reserved for a man and a woman so the love between people of the same sex was seen as inferior and invalid until 2015.

If we observe the way we treat people in bigger bodies today, it echoes each one of these constructs I just mentioned. We live in a world where we are told that bodies that are not a BMI of 19-24 are unhealthy. We are told that bigger bodies are less worthy of respect, acceptance and love. We are told that we should, at all costs, pursue thinness and the shrinking of our body size.

Weight stigma and fatphobia exists, it's called sizeism and it is just as real as racisms and sexism. It is wrong that our society treats people differently based on their weight, just like it is wrong to treat people differently based on their race, gender or sexual orientation.

Weight based discrimination comes from employers, health care professionals, educators, and even our family members. It has widespread implications on the physical and psychological health of us all. This judgement of body shapes inhibits our ability to get the health care services we need, leaves us engaging in unhealthy eating behaviors like eating disorders, and makes us avoid physical activity in fear of being made fun of. It keeps us from fully engaging in and living our lives on many other levels as well.

Now imagine if Elizabeth Cady Stanton didn't voice her discontent with women's rights under the new democracy in America back in 1848?

(107) Imagine if Martin Luther King Jr. just decided to be complicit in the mistreat of people based on skin color. What if he didn't voice his dream for a more fair and civil world in 1963? Progress does not get made by accepting the status quo. Progress is made by standing up for what you believe in and is true, regardless of what others may believe or we are told is the truth.

This is an open invitation to stand up for your body no matter what it looks like. It is valid, worthy, healthy, whole, beautiful, loveable and respectable just the way it is. I encourage you to stop fighting against yourself and start fighting against this injustice against body diversity.

Engage in the Discovery Process

At the end of each chapter I included some action steps for you to take to help you discover your Body Wisdom. If you haven't been doing them as you've read through the book I encourage you to do them now over the next week or month or however long it takes. Use what you learn to start to understand what is happening in your body and then decode the information it sends you.

My Body Wisdom Pillars

Over the last 7 years I have developed an intimate relationship with my body and mind. I have been able to witness a shift in my mental and emotional state by honoring my body with foods that make it feel good. At the same time, I have experience a shift in my digestion by practicing body acceptance and self-love which has decreased my anxiety and stress.

Below are my pillars, or truths, for honoring my Body Wisdom

80/20 Rule:
The 80/20 rule, aka the Pareto principle, states that roughly 80% of the events come from 20% of the causes.(108) It has been adopted

in business management stating that 80% of profits come from 20% of clients/customers. Interestingly enough, the 80/20 principle has also been found true in several areas in life whereby 80% of the world's wealth is in the hands of 20% of the world's population.

Since being one way 100% of the time is really challenging if not impossible, I have adopted the 80/20 principle into many areas of my life to help me achieve balance; beauty products, cleaning products, clothing (used vs new), what area I focus on in my business, and the way I eat.

I strive to eat SOUL food 80% of the time and the other 20% of the time I eat whatever I want that doesn't fall into the SOUL category. I never feel deprived nor do I really track or count my food with any detail but I use it as a loose framework to operate within.

Liquids:

I drink water about 80% of the time. And 20% of the time I have juice, soda water like La Croix, alcohol, tea or coffee. I occasionally have a kombucha, and always pass on sports drinks and soda- those are just not really my thing.

Movement:

Moving our body is one of the pillars of a healthy life. But it doesn't have to be strenuous or taxing to our body. And it doesn't even have to necessarily be a "workout" to be beneficial. Everything from parking in the back of the parking lot and walking to the store to cleaning our house with extra vigor or climbing stairs when possible all count as valuable movement and activity.

That being said, sweating and increasing our heart rate is beneficial for so many reasons. Sweating regenerates and detoxifies the skin. It helps with metabolism, decreases our risk for various disease, strengthens our bones and muscles, and improves our mood and mental health. I always tell my clients that 10 minutes is still better than no minutes. Get in movement of some kind everyday be it a walk, hike, some light yoga in your room or a short bike ride. And be on the lookout for how you can add some extra activity throughout the day.

While I do not work out or exercise every day, I am active everyday by walking around, going for walks, and dancing while cooking dinner. Additionally, I do not put pressure on myself to work out excessively or on any type of consistent basis. Rather, I let my body guide me and tell me what it needs. On days when I am stressed, I will almost always go for a run or a hike because it helps relieve my anxiety. Other days, I can just tell that my body wants to move more, so I listen. This not only removes the whole "work" part of working out, but makes it more about having fun as opposed to exercise being just another item on my to-do list.

Move because it feels good, not because it is a punishment for what you ate or because you "should."

I always look from the perspective of authentic inspiration to take care of my body, not shameful obligation because I'm "bad" if I don't.

Self-Care

Prioritizing self-care is as important for a healthy and happy balanced life as eating SOUL-food, drinking water, and moving your body. It's impossible to pour from an empty cup, so be sure to fill yours up when it's getting low. I personally show myself some love by getting my nails done. In fact, few things make me feel as refreshed like a fresh coat of nail polish. Also taking myself out for a green juice, a glass of wine, or putting on a face mask are all forms of self-care that are meaningful for me. Even putting on a great podcast and getting out for a walk is a great way to not only stimulate your mind and take a break from looking at a screen, but also a fantastic way to move your body. Other ideas include taking a luxurious bubble bath, cooking yourself a meal, getting a massage, making a cup of golden milk or tea, doing some gentle yoga, or calling up a friend to talk through whatever is on your mind. Whatever it is you feel drawn to, take some time out for yourself to do it.

Journaling and Gratitude

Part of my morning routine includes spending 5 or so minutes writing in my gratitude journal. I simply put the date and list around 3-5 things I am grateful for. Studies show that when we are practicing gratitude regularly, we can actually change our brain chemistry and improve our health, so why not give this a try?[109] Fear and gratitude are opposing actions on a physiological level, so choosing to be grateful literally interrupts anxiety. I don't often journal beyond 3-5 things that I am grateful for, but if this form of expression calls to you then I encourage you to journal as much as you need.

Meditation

Meditation is a powerful mental break and a little goes a long way. I meditate almost every day. Sometimes I am rushed in the morning and don't give myself enough time, but as little as 10 minutes can have a profound impact on how my day goes. I find that I have more mental clarity, a strong ability to focus, am less stressed and am less reactive when I prioritize my morning meditation. It really is a phenomenal tool. Even if you do not enjoy meditation it still is beneficial. If you're new check out the apps Headspace or Calm.

Positive Affirmations

Positive affirmations play a huge role in my life. It's not uncommon for me to have sticky notes on my mirror or desk with little reminders to stay connected to my highest self. There is so much negativity in the world and every fiber of my being believes that optimism and positivity is always the best route to take. That doesn't mean I don't deal with reality, rather I make conscious ever to see the bright side. Plus our thoughts create our world and effect how we show up each day. I know that when I tell myself I look beautiful, my nervous system respond and life is more enjoyable then if I berate myself. Try it. Pick a few and repeat them as needed.

FUN

Try to do one thing a week that is just for PURE FUN. This can be anything that you enjoy that you don't always make time for. Life goes by really fast and it's so important to take time aside to simply enjoy being alive. I love to have fun by going to music festivals like Coachella, trying a new restaurant, taking bike rides in a new part of the city, watching some Netflix, or vision boarding! As we grow up sometimes we forget that life is about more than just our careers and to-do lists.

Each of us has an inner spirit and child that needs to be nurtured. In fact, I find that I am always more creative, inspired and passion driven after allowing myself to just enjoy life and take the pressure off of myself to be so productive. We live in a society that praises the hustle, the grind, and being busy.

One of the best lessons I have learned as a soul-driven entrepreneur is that always being busy really isn't all it's cut out to be and often leads to a burn out. Playing and having fun is often the most productive thing I can do for myself. So remember have fun, be silly, and get connected to what brings you joy.

A Little Recap:
1. **Define "Health" for Yourself**
2. **Listen to Your Body**
3. **Stand Up for Your Body**
4. **Trust Your Body**
5. **Engage in the Discovery Process**
6. **Create Your Own Body Wisdom Pillars**

14
EASY NOURISHING RECIPES

"There is no sincerer love than the love of food"

— George Bernard Shaw

No book about food, health and nourishing our bodies would be complete without some recipes, right? Right!

Below are some easy ones for you to try. The majority are vegetarian and vegan, simply because I do eat mostly plants but also to be honest, I am pretty bad at preparing meat. Typically my boyfriend does all of that and so I haven't really developed the skill. That said at the end of this chapter are some of my absolute favorite cookbooks and blogs that include several more qualified people to share recipes with a variety of ingredients!

Happy cooking and happy eating!

BREAKFAST

Nut Butter Strawberry Overnight Oats

Serves 2 | 5 minute prep with 6 hours in the fridge to set | Total 6hr 5m

Ingredients

- 1 cup unsweetened almond milk
- 2 tbsp chia seeds
- 4 tbsp peanut or Almond butter,
- 2 tbsp maple syrup, optional
- 1 cup rolled oats
- 1 cup sliced strawberries

Directions:

In a small bowl combine all the ingredients, except the strawberries and stir around to mix together slightly. Then in a mason jar or container layer some of the oat mixture, then half the strawberries, then the rest of the oat mixture followed by the remaining strawberries on top. Cover with a lid or plastic wrap and leave the fridge for 6 hours or overnight. This keeps well for 2 days in the fridge so feel free to make a couple in advance to save time.

Sweet Potato with Nutella & Fresh Fruit

Serves 2 | 10 minute prep | 20 minutes cook

Ingredients

- 2 sweet potato halves, roasted
- 2 banana, slices
- 1/2 cup berries

- ▸ 4 tbsp Nutella or nut butter
- ▸ 1 tbsp hemp seeds
- ▸ 1 lemon, juiced (optional)

Directions:

Preheat oven to 400f. Cut sweet potatoes in half and lay cut side down on try. Roast for 15-20 minutes until soft. Layer on Nutella or nut butter, fresh berries, banana, hemp seeds and lemon juice. To save on time in the morning you can roast the sweet potatoes the night before if desired.

Savory Oats with Mushroom, Spinach and a fried egg

Serves 2 | 5 min prep | cook time: 13 minutes

Ingredients:

- ▸ 2 tbsp olive oil
- ▸ 1/2 small onion, diced
- ▸ 2 garlic clove, minced
- ▸ 10 cremini mushrooms, sliced
- ▸ 1-2 cups spinach
- ▸ 1 cup rolled oats
- ▸ 1 1/2 cup vegetable broth
- ▸ 2 fried eggs, preferably organic pasture raised
- ▸ 12 cherry tomatoes, halved
- ▸ ½ avocado slices

Directions

In a small cast iron skillet heat oil over medium. Once hot add in the onion and sauté for 3 minutes. Add a pinch of pink salt and the garlic. Add the mushrooms and sauté for 3 minutes, adding a small pinch a salt. Cook for

30 seconds and then add in the oats and the vegetable broth. Cover with a lid. Stir the vegetable broth occasionally until the oats are cooked, about 7 minutes. Then stir the spinach and stir until it wilts. Transfer to a serving bowl and top with the fried egg, fresh cherry tomatoes and avocados.

The Basic Smoothie

Serves 1 | 5 min prep

Ingredients:

- 1 frozen banana
- 1 cup almond milk
- 2 tbsp peanut butter
- 1/4 cup oats
- 1 scoop vanilla or chocolate protein powder (optional)
- 2 tbsp chia seeds
- 1 cup spinach
- (ice if banana not frozen)

Directions:

Combine all ingredients in a blender and blend until smooth. Pour into a glass and enjoy

Peanut Butter Banana Overnight Oats

Serves 2 | 5 minute prep with 6 hours in the fridge to set | Total 6hr 5m

Ingredients

- 1 ½ cup unsweetened almond milk
- 4 tbsp peanut butter
- 2 tbsp chia seeds

- 1 ½ cup rolled oats
- 1 banana, peeled, sliced in coins

Directions:

In a small bowl combine all the ingredients except the fruit and stir around to mix. Then in a mason jar layer some of the oat mix, then half the banana, then the rest of the oat mixture. Repeat for second serving.

Cover with a lid or plastic wrap and leave the fridge for 6 hours or overnight.

Marinated Tomato Avocado Toast

Serves 2 | 20 minute prep

Ingredients:

- 1 cup cherry tomatoes, sliced in half
- 3 tbsp balsamic vinegar
- 3 tbsp olive oil
- ¼ tsp garlic powder
- Pink salt & pepper to taste
- 2 slices of your favorite bread, toasted
- 2 tbsp mayo, optional
- 1 ripe avocado, sliced

Directions:

Add the sliced tomatoes to a small bowl and add the vinegar, olive oil, garlic powder, pink salt and pepper. Mix around and let sit for 12 minutes to marinate. You can do this the night before and leave overnight as well if you want to save time in the morning.

Then toast bread in the toaster or the oven. Spread vegan mayo on each slice of bread, followed by ½ avocado on each. Mash the avocado with the back of a fork and then top with the tomatoes.

Green Giant Smoothie

Serves 2 | 5 minute prep

Ingredients:

- 1 banana, frozen
- 1 cucumber
- 2 cups spinach
- 2 green apples, peeled, seeded and chopped
- 2 cups coconut water, or water
- 4-6 romaine leaves

Directions:

Add everything into a blender and turn on high.

Fluffy Vegan Pancakes

Serves 2 | 5 minutes Prep | 10 Minutes cook

Ingredients:

- ½ cup unsweetened apple sauce
- 1 ¼ cup oat flour (rolled oats ground up in a blender)
- ½ cup almond milk
- 2 tsp lemon juice
- 2 tbsp maple syrup
- 1 tsp baking powder
- 1 tsp baking soda
- 1 tsp vanilla extract
- 1/8 tsp cinnamon (optional)
- 1 tbsp coconut oil

To Serve:
- ¼ cup maple syrup for topping
- 1 banana, sliced, for topping

Directions:

Combine all ingredients in a blender and blend until combined. If you do not already have the oat flour, blend that first into flour and then add the ingredients. DO NOT over blend. Heat a non-stick skillet over medium high heat. Add coconut oil and coat the pan evenly.

Pour about a 1/3 cup measurement of batter into the pan. Since it is quite thick, spread it out into a circle with a spoon. Not your finger. You don't want to burn yourself. Cook for 2-3 minutes on the first side and when the spatula slides under it easily, flip and cook on the other side. Continue until batter is done. Makes 4-6 pancakes. Top with maple syrup and banana.

LUNCH

Avocado Chickpea Salad Sandwich

Serves 2 | Prep 10 minutes

Ingredients:

- 1-15-ounce can of garbanzo bean. Rinsed and drained
- 1 ripe avocado, mashed
- ½ small red onion, diced
- 1 lime, juice
- ½ tsp garlic powder
- ¼ tsp chili powder
- 1/8 tsp Salt, more to taste
- 1 tomato, sliced
- 4 slices of bread

Directions:

Add the chickpeas to a bowl and mash with the back of a fork. Then add in the avocado and mash a bit more. Then add the lime juice, red onion, garlic powder and salt. Mix again. Toast your bread and then layer the garbanzo bean mix and tomato slices between two piece of the bread to make a sandwich.

Easy Greek Salad

Serves 2 | prep 15

Dressing:

- 6 tbsp olive oil
- 4 tbsp lemon juice
- 1/8 tsp garlic powder

- 1/8 tsp dried oregano
- 1/8 tsp Pink salt and pepper

Salad:
- 4 cups chopped salad greens
- 1 cup cherry tomatoes, sliced in half
- ½ cup Kalamata olives
- 2 Persian cucumbers sliced
- 1 avocado, cubed
- 1 tbsp nuts of choice, optional
- Pinch hemp seeds, for garnish

Directions:

Add salad dressing ingredients into a bowl and combine well. Set aside. Prepare salad ingredients as stated above. Divide amongst two bowls and cover with the dressing. Add nuts and hemp seeds if desired for protein and health benefits.

Three Bean Salad

Serves 2 | Prep 5 mins

Ingredients:

- 1 can garbanzo beans
- 1 can black beans
- 1 can pinto/kidney/ white bean (your choice
- ½ red onion, diced
- 1 cup Persian cucumber, chopped

Dressing:
- ½ cup balsamic vinegar
- ½ cup olive oil
- 1-2 tsp maple syrup (optional)
- 1/8 tsp pink salt & Black pepper, to taste

Directions

Rinse and drain all the beans. Add to a bowl with the red onion and cucumber. Add all the dressing ingredients to a jar and with a lid and shake to combine. Then pour on top of the bean salad. Let marinate for 30 minutes in the fridge then serve.

The Easy Veggie Sandwich

Serves 2 | Prep 5 minutes

Ingredients:

- ▶ 4 slices of our favorite bread, toasted
- ▶ 1 roma tomato, sliced
- ▶ 2 Persian cucumber sliced in thick ribbons, horizontally
- ▶ ½ avocado, sliced
- ▶ 2 radish, thinly sliced (optional)
- ▶ ½ lime, juiced
- ▶ ¼ tsp garlic powder
- ▶ 2 tbsp mayo, hummus or grass-fed butter
- ▶ ¼ cup sprouts, microgreens or fresh herbs (whatever you have on hand)

Directions:

Toast the bread. Meanwhile prep ingredients as stated above. Layer the mayo on one side of each piece of bread. Then the avocado and add the lime juice and garlic powder. Then add the herbs, tomato, cucumber and radish if using. Top with the other piece of bread.

Lemon Kale Chickpea Avocado Salad

Serves 2 | 15 minute prep |

Lemon Dressing:
- ▸ 2 tbsp lemon juice
- ▸ 1 garlic clove, minced
- ▸ ½ tsp pink salt
- ▸ 1/8 tsp black pepper
- ▸ ¼ cup extra virgin olive oil

Salad:
- ▸ 8 cups kale, chopped
- ▸ 1 15-ounce can of garbanzo beans, rinsed and drained
- ▸ 1 ripe avocado diced

Directions:

Add the dressing ingredients into a bowl. Whisk to combine well. Add the dressing to a large bowl with the kale and massage with your hands for a couple of minutes. Then add the chickpeas and avocado. Toss to coat.

White Bean Salad Pita Pockets

Serves 2 | 15 minute prep

Dressing:
- ▸ 1/4 cup vegan yogurt, unsweetened plain
- ▸ 2 tbsp lemon juice
- ▸ 1/2 tsp dijon mustard
- ▸ ¼ tsp pink salt
- ▸ 1/8 tsp black pepper

White bean salad:
- ▸ 1-15 ounce can of white beans
- ▸ ½ cup cucumber, diced
- ▸ ¼ cup red bell pepper, diced
- ▸ 1 green onion, sliced

For Serving:
- 2 pita pockets
- 2 leaves of romaine lettuce

Directions:

In a medium bowl, whisk all the dressing ingredients together until well combined. Then add all the prepped veggies ingredients into the bowl and mix. Then taste it to see if it needs more salt or lemon juice for flavor. Gently open the pita pockets and put a piece of lettuce in each. Then spoon in the white bean salad mixture. Enjoy.

7 Layer Burrito Salad

Serves 2 | 15 minute prep

Ingredients:

- 1-15-ounce can of refried beans (pinto or black)
- 1/2 cup red onion, diced
- 1 cup corn kernels, frozen
- 1 cup tomatoes, diced
- 1 cup red bell pepper, diced
- 1 avocado, cubed
- 2 romaine hearts, chopped
- 2 limes, juiced
- 1 tsp garlic powder

Ingredients:

In a bowl or casserole square dish, layer the refried beans, using a spoon to spread out, then add the red onion, corn, tomatoes, red bell pepper, avocado and the romaine lettuce. Squeeze on the lime juice and sprinkle on the garlic powder and dig in. Option to serve with chips.

BBQ Chickpea Salad

Serves 2 | 15 minute prep

Salad:

- 1 15-ounce can of garbanzo beans
- ¼ cup bbq sauce, store bought
- 2 romaine hearts, chopped
- ½ cup tomato, diced
- 1 cup cucumber, sliced
- 1 cup corn kernels, frozen and defrosted
- ¼ cup diced red onion
- 1 avocado, cubed

Dressing:

- 1 tbsp tahini
- 2 limes juiced
- 1 tbsp olive oil
- ¼ tsp garlic powder
- ¼ tsp salt
- 1-2 tbsp water, if desired for consistency
- 2 lime wedges, for serving.

Directions:

Make the dressing by combining everything in a small bowl and whisk to combine. In a small bowl add the garbanzo beans and the bbq sauce. Toss to coat. Set aside. Then in two salad bowls divide up the romaine, tomatoes, cucumbers, corn, red onion and avocado. Top with the bbq garbanzo beans drizzle on the dressing. Serve with a lime wedge.

DINNER

Loaded Sweet Potatoes with Spiced Black Beans and Avocado

Serves 2 | Prep 5 minutes |28 mins

Ingredients:

- 2 sweet potatoes, rinsed and halved
- 1 -15 ounce can of black beans, rinsed and drained
- 2 tbsp coconut oil
- 1/2 tsp cumin
- 1/2 tsp garlic powder
- 1/8 tsp chili powder
- ¼ tsp pink salt, to taste
- 1 avocado, mashed or sliced
- 1 lime, juiced
- 1 tsp nutritional yeast
- ¼ tsp hemp seeds
- ¼ tsp red pepper flakes

Directions:

Preheat oven to 400 degrees F and line a baking sheet with parchment paper. Brush with olive oil and place face down on the baking sheet. Roast for 25-28 minutes. Mix the black beans with the garlic powder, cumin and chili. Season with salt and pepper. Once the potatoes are done, layer one with the black beans, avocado, lime juice and garnish with nutritional yeast, hemp seeds, red pepper flakes and pink salt.

Cauliflower Fried Rice:

Serves 2 | Prep 10 minutes | Cook 13 minutes

Ingredients:

- ▸ 2 scrambled eggs, preferably pasture raised organic
- ▸ 1 tbsp sesame oil
- ▸ 2 garlic cloves, minced
- ▸ 2 carrots, peeled and diced
- ▸ ½ head cauliflower, riced (about 4-5 cups)
- ▸ ½ tsp red pepper flakes
- ▸ 2 green onions
- ▸ ½ cup frozen peas
- ▸ ½ cup frozen corn
- ▸ 2 tbsp tamari
- ▸ 1 tbsp cashews, for garnish
- ▸ 1/8 tsp sesame seeds for garnish

Directions:

To rice the cauliflower you can put it in a food processor or chop finely with a knife. Heat sesame oil over medium high heat in a large pan. Add the garlic and stir for 30 seconds. Then add the carrots and cook for 3 minutes. Season with pink salt. Then add the red pepper flakes, green onions, cauliflower, peas, corn and soy sauce. Cook for 10 minutes or until cauliflower is tender. Stir in the eggs and serve immediately. Garnish with cashews or sesame seeds if desired. Consider adding a pasture raised fried egg on top too!

Pasta & Peas with Alfredo Sauce:

Serves 2 | Prep 10 minutes | cook 10 minutes

Ingredients

- ▶ 4-5 ounces gluten free pasta
- ▶ 1 cup cashews, soaked in hot water for 30 minutes
- ▶ 2 garlic cloves, minced
- ▶ 3 tbsp nutritional yeast
- ▶ ¼ tsp red pepper flakes
- ▶ ¼ tsp garlic powder
- ▶ 1 lemon, juiced
- ▶ Water or unsweetened plain almond milk, as needed to thin to desired consistency
- ▶ 1 cup frozen peas

Directions

Add past to a large pot of boiling water and cook following package instructions. Add the cashews, garlic, nutritional yeast and lemon juice to a blender. Turn on high. Scrape down the sides a couple of times as needed. Then add almond milk or water starting with 1-2 tbsp at a time until sauce is thick and at desired consistency. Adjust the flavors by adding more salt if the flavor is dull, nutritional yeast for more cheese flavor, lemon for more brightness. Defrost the peas under hot running water. Add the sauce, pasta and peas to a bowl. Toss to combine and serve with extra nutritional yeast and red pepper flakes on top.

Rice and Beans Buddha Bowl

Serves 2 | 15 minute prep | 20 minutes cook

Ingredients:

- ▶ 1 cup brown rice
- ▶ 2 cups water or vegetable broth
- ▶ 1 15-ounce cans black beans
- ▶ 4 cups kale
- ▶ ½ avocado, sliced
- ▶ 2 tbsp hemp seeds

Sauce:
- ▶ 2 cups tahini
- ▶ 1 cup lemon juiced
- ▶ 2 tbsp fresh dill or 1 tbsp dried dill

Directions:

Bring the two cups of water and rice to a bowl. Then cover and lower to a simmer. Cook according to package instructions.

Over medium heat, warm up a saucepan and add the black beans. Stir around for 3-4 minutes until warm. Remove and set side. Then add the kale and gently sauté until it starts to wilt, about 2-3 minutes. Mix the tahini, lemon juice and dill together in a small bowl. Then layer the cooked rice, black beans, kale and avocado in a bowl. Top with the tahini sauce and hemp seeds.

Ginger Peanut Noodle Bowl

Serves 2 | 5 minute prep | 10 minutes cooking

Peanut Dressing:

- ▶ 2 tbsp toasted sesame oil
- ▶ 2 tbsp salted peanut butter
- ▶ 2 tbsp maple syrup, agave or honey
- ▶ 1 tbsp soy sauce or tamari
- ▶ 1 lime, juiced
- ▶ 1 tsp fresh grated ginger
- ▶ ¼ tsp very hot water, if the sauce is too thick

Noodle Bowl:

- ▶ 2 cups cooked rice noodles
- ▶ ½ cup organic extra firm tofu, patted dry and cut into cubes
- ▶ ½ cup carrots, chopped into matchsticks
- ▶ ½ cup cucumber, chopped into matchsticks
- ▶ ½ cup green onion
- ▶ ½ cup basil, chopped
- ▶ 2 tbsp sriracha (optional)

Directions:

Prepare noodles according to package instructions. Generally, place the noodles in a bowl, pour boiling water on top and let sit for 10 minutes before draining. Rice noodles like this can be found at Asian markets or often in the Asian section of your local supermarket. If you cannot find rice noodles, soba or ramen noodles work great as well.

Make the peanut dressing by combining all ingredients together in a bowl and whisk until smooth. You can use store bought too if you prefer.

Chop the tofu into cubes. (sub cooked pasture raised chicken if desired)

Once the noodles are done add to a bowl layer with the tofu, carrots, green onions and sauce. Mix well and then top with fresh basil and sriracha if using.

Easy Pasta with Broccoli

Serves 2 | 10 minute prep | 15 minutes cook

Ingredients:

Pasta:
- ▶ 6 cups pasta shells, your favorite store bought brand
- ▶ 1 tbsp olive oil
- ▶ 1 cup onion, diced
- ▶ 2 garlic cloves, minded
- ▶ 4 cups broccoli, chopped into small bite sized florets
- ▶ ¼ cup vegan parmesan cheese (recipe below)

Sauce:
- ▶ 2 tbsp cooking liquid used for the pasta
- ▶ ½ cup lemon juice
- ▶ ½ cup olive oil
- ▶ ½ tsp garlic powder
- ▶ ½ tsp salt
- ▶ ¼ tsp black pepper

Vegan Parmesan Cheese (makes more than you need, save for later)
- ▶ 1 cup cashews
- ▶ 1 tbsp hemp seeds
- ▶ ½ cup nutritional yeast
- ▶ ¾ tsp salt
- ▶ ½ tsp garlic powder

Parmesan Cheese Directions: Combine everything in a blender and pulse until it resembles cheese.

Directions:

Bring a pot of boiling water to a bowl. Add some salt and the pasta. Cook according to package instructions.

Then heat up a large frying pan over medium high. Add the oil and once hot toss in the onions. Cook for 3-4 minutes until translucent. Lower to medium, add the garlic and stir around for 30 seconds. Then add in the broccoli and cook for 5-6 minutes until fork tender. Stirring occasionally.

Once the pasta is done, remove 2 tbsp of the cooking liquid and add it to a large bowl that you will use for the pasta. Drain the pasta. Then add in the remaining sauce ingredients to the bowl. Whisk to combine and then add in the pasta and broccoli. Top with parmesan cheese.

SNACKS

Raw PB & J Balls

Makes 7 balls | 12 minutes

Ingredients:

- ¼ cup peanut butter, creamy salted
- 2 tbsp maple syrup
- 1/3 cup rolled oats
- 1 tbsp flaxseed meal or ground chia seeds
- 1 tbsp dried fruit (cranberries, raisins, blueberries) *Can sub chocolate chips instead

Directions:

In a small bowl combine everything in a bowl and mix well. If too dry add more peanut butter or maple syrup. If to sticky or wet, add more rolled oats of flaxseed meal. Chill in the fridge for 5 minutes and then roll out into balls. Keeps well for 1 7 days in fridge or a month in the freezer.

Garlic Walnuts

Serves 2 | 10 minutes

Ingredients:

- 2 tbsp olive oil
- 1 tsp garlic powder
- 1 cup walnuts
- ¼ tsp Pink salt, more to taste

Directions:

In a cast iron skillet, heat olive oil over medium. Add in the garlic powder and stir for 30 seconds then add the walnuts. Stir to coat and toss occasionally for 5-7 minutes until fragrant and toasty. Season with pink salt.

Baked Sweet Potato Chips

Serves 2 | Prep 10 Minutes | Cook 2 hours

Ingredients:

- ▸ 1 sweet potato
- ▸ 1 tbsp olive or coconut oil
- ▸ ¼ tsp salt

Directions:

Preheat oven to 250f. Rinse and dry potato. Slice as thin and uniformly as possible. Use a mandolin if you have one otherwise a sharp knife works. BE CAREFUL! If not super thin they won't crisp up as well but will still be tasty. Toss with the oil and salt. Lay in a single layer on a baking sheet and bake for 2 hours flipping at the 1 hour mark. Rotate the try as well for more even cooking. Remove and let rest for 10 minutes so they can crisp up more in the air. Serve immediately.

Sweet Toast:

Serves 2 | Prep 5 minutes

Ingredients:

- ▸ 2 slices organic bread of choice
- ▸ 6 tbsp vegan yogurt of choice

- ▸ 2 apricots, quartered
- ▸ 1 handful fresh raspberries
- ▸ ½ tsp Cinnamon sugar

Directions:

Toast bread in a toaster or oven. Spread on the yogurt and layer with fruit and finish with cinnamon sugar.

Nut Butter Dates and Banana

Serves 2 | 5 minute prep

Ingredients:

- ▸ 6 dates, pitted
- ▸ 2 tbsp almond butter
- ▸ ¼ banana, cut into coins

Directions:

Gently remove the pit from the dates and open up the date. Spoon in nut butter and top each date with a banana slice

Cheesy Kale Chips

Serves 2 | 4 minute prep | 15 minutes cook

Ingredients:

- ▸ 6 cups kale leaves, de-stemmed and cut into bite sized pieces
- ▸ 2 tbsp olive oil
- ▸ 2 tbsp nutritional yeast
- ▸ 1 tsp pink salt

Directions:

Preheat oven to 375 F. Wash and pat dry the kale, remove the stems and cut into bite sized pieces. Then drizzle with olive oil and use your hands to mix and coat the leaves. Then lay out in a single layer on a baking sheet. You might have to use to baking sheets. Then sprinkle with the nutritional yeast and salt. Put in the oven and roast for 10-15 minutes until almost crunchy. Remove from the oven and let sit out for 3-5 minutes. They will crisp up more in the air.

Easy Chip Dip

Serves 2 | 10 minute prep |5 minute cook

Ingredients:

- ▶ 1-15-ounce of refried beans (pinto or black)
- ▶ 1 cup salsa, store bought
- ▶ ½ avocado, cubed

To Serve:
- ▶ 6 cups corn chips

Directions:

Open the can of beans and heat up in a skillet or the microwave for a couple of minutes. Then in a medium bowl add the beans, salsa and avocado. Stir to combine. Dip some chips in it.

The Best Sweet Potato Fries Ever

Serves 2 | 10 minute prep | 35-45 minute cook

Ingredients:

- ▶ 2 large sweet potatoes, cut into steak fries, skin on
- ▶ 3-4 tbsp coconut oil
- ▶ Pink salt
- ▶ cinnamon

Directions:

Preheat oven to 450 degrees F. Lay the sweet potato fries across to sheet pans. Generously coat with the coconut oil and spices. Toss to coat. Roast until crispy and almost burnt on the side that touches the pan.

Serve with my Cashew Vegan Caesar Dressing

Caesar Dressing: (makes 2 cups dressing)

Ingredients:

- ▶ 1 cup raw cashews, soaked in hot water for 30 minutes or room temp for 3 hours
- ▶ 1/2 cup extra virgin olive oil
- ▶ 4 tbsp lemon juice
- ▶ 4 tbsp filtered water
- ▶ 2 large garlic
- ▶ 2 tbsp vegan Worcestershire sauce
- ▶ 2 tbsp capers
- ▶ 2 tbsp nutritional yeast
- ▶ 3 tsp pink salt
- ▶ 2 tsp garlic powder
- ▶ 1 tsp Dijon mustard.

Directions:

Blend everything in a high speed blender

Some other great resources for you to check out for recipes:

Cookbooks:

1. *Gjelina: Cooking from Venice, California* by Travis Lett
2. *Salt, Fat, Acid, Heat: Mastering the Elements of Good Cooking* by Samin Nosrat
3. *The Love and Lemons Cookbook: An Apple-to-Zucchini Celebration of Impromptu Cooking* by Jeanine Donofrio
4. *The Lemonade Cookbook: Southern California Comfort Food from L.A.'s Favorite Modern Cafeteria* by Alan Jackson and JoAnn Cianciulli
5. *Bulletproof Cookbook* by Dave Aspery

Blogs:

1. What's Gaby Cooking: https://whatsgabycooking.com/
2. Nom Nom Paleo: https://nomnompaleo.com/
3. The Minimalist Baker: https://minimalistbaker.com/
4. Paleo Running Mamma https://www.paleorunningmomma.com/
5. Guac My Life https://www.guacmylife.com/
6. Food 52 https://food52.com/
7. Week Night Bite https://www.weeknightbite.com/
8. What Great Grandma Ate https://whatgreatgrandmaate.com/

For more information and to keep up on my blog, coaching articles and recipes, visit www.caraskitchen.net and subscribe to my newsletter. You can also find me on:

Instagram: @caraskitchen

Youtube: Caras Kitchen

Facebook: https://www.facebook.com/carainthekitchen

And with that babes, I am out! Thank you so much, I am truly grateful and humbled by you reading this book. I hope it helps you connect more deeply to your beautiful body machine.

Xo C

BIBLIOGRAPHY

1. *Intuitive Eating* by Evelyn Tribole and Elyse Resch
   http://www.intuitiveeating.org/
2. *Health at Every Size* by Linda Bacon
   https://haescommunity.com/
   https://lindabacon.org/
3. *The China Study* By T. Colin Campbell
   https://nutritionstudies.org/
4. *Eating in the Light of the Moon* By Dr. Anita Johnson
   https://dranitajohnston.com/
5. *Why Diets Make us Fat* By Dr. Sandra Aamodt
   http://www.sandraaamodt.com

NOTES AND REFERENCES

1. Moshe Shike, Ashley S. Doane, Lianne Russo, Rafael Cabal, Jorge S. Reis-Filho, William Gerald, Hiram Cody, Raya Khanin, Jacqueline Bromberg, Larry Norton; The Effects of Soy Supplementation on Gene Expression in Breast Cancer: A Randomized Placebo-Controlled Study, *JNCI: Journal of the National Cancer Institute*, Volume 106, Issue 9, 1 September 2014, dju189, https://doi.org/10.1093/jnci/dju189

2. Robinson, Kara Mayer., Cassoobhoy, Arefa., MD, MPH, *Protein and Cholesterol*, May 16, 2014 http://www.webmd.com/cholesterol-management/features/soy-and-cholesterol#1

3. Grube B, Chong PW, Lau KZ, Orzechowski HD. A natural fiber complex reduces body weight in the overweight and obese: a double-blind, randomized, placebo-controlled study. *Obesity (Silver Spring)*. 2013;21:58-64. 2. Grube B, Chong PW, Alt F, Uebelhack R. Weight maintenance with Litramine (IQP-G-002AS): a 24-week double-blind, randomized, placebo-controlled study. *J Obes*. 2015;2015:1 https://www.multivu.com/players/English/8215151-the-truth-about-weight-loss-national-survey/

4. Bacon, Linda., *Health at Every Size*. Dallas: BenBella, 2008. Print

5. Johnson, Dr. Anita. *Eating in the Light of the Moon*. Carlsbad: Gurze Books, 2000. Print

6. Tory Dube — torybue.com

7. Hyman, Dr. Mark., *5 Things We Learned from the Broken Brain Docuseries*, 2007, http://drhyman.com/blog/2017/10/27/5-things-learned-broken-brain-docuseries/

8. https://adaa.org/about-adaa/press-room/facts-statistics

9. Southwest Institute of Healing Arts, Phoenix, Arizona, Holistic Nutrition

10. Ferguson, James M., MD., *SSRI Antidepressant Medications: Adverse Effects and Tolerability*, 2001 https://www.ncbi.nlm.nih.gov/pmc/articles/PMC181155/

11. Stoller-Conraw, Jessica., *Microbes Help Produce Serotonin in Gut*, 04/09/2015 http://www.caltech.edu/news/microbes-help-produce-serotonin-gut-46495

12. Hadhazy, Adam., *Think Twice: How the Gut's "Second Brain" Influences Mood and Well-Being*, 02/12/2010 https://www.scientificamerican.com/article/gut-second-brain/

13. Kaslow, Jeremy E., MD., *Neurotransmitter Repletion*, http://www.drkaslow.com/html/neurotransmitter_repletion.html

14. Smith, Lori., Wilson, Debra Rose., PhD., *10 Most Common Birth Control Pll Side Effects*. 01/29/2018., https://www.medicalnewstoday.com/articles/290196.php

15. Adams, Kelly M., Lindell, Karen C., Kohlmeier, Martin., Zeisel, Steven H., *Status of Nutrition Education in Medical Schools* 2008 https://www.ncbi.nlm.nih.gov/pmc/articles/PMC2430660/

16. Harvard Health Publishing, *Butter vs. Margarine* https://www.health.harvard.edu/nutrition/butter-vs-margarine

17. O'Reilly, Kevin B., 4 Reasons Why Health Coaching Works. 01/12/2017 https://wire.ama-assn.org/practice-management/4-reasons-why-health-coaching-works

18. Leveque, Kelly., Table 1 *Body Love*, 2017, Harpercollins

19. Shears, Gewnyth., *S.O.U.L Food.* 04/26/2016 https://www.baumancollege.org/soul/

20. Howell, Elizabeth., *How Long Have Humans Been On Earth*. 01/19/2015 https://www.universetoday.com/38125/how-long-have-humans-been-on-earth/

21. Gold, Mary V., *Organic Production/Organic Food: Information* June 2007, Reviewed April 2016. https://www.nal.usda.gov/afsic/organic-productionorganic-food-information-access-tools

22. Baranski, M. et al. *Study Finds Significant Differences Between Organic and Non-Organic Food.* British Journal of Nutrition, 07/15/2015 https://hygeia-analytics.com/2016/12/14/press-release-new-study-finds-significant-differences-between-organic-and-non-organic-food/

23. Gold, Mary V., *Organic Production/Organic Food: Information* June 2007, Reviewed April 2016. https://www.nal.usda.gov/afsic/organic-productionorganic-food-information-access-tools

24. Marrett, Diane M., *Maximizing the Nutritional Value of Fruits and Vegetables*. http://www.fruitandvegetable.ucdavis.edu/files/197179.pdf

25. Kim, Evelyn., *Processed Food: A 2-Million-Year History. 09/01/2013.* https://www.scientificamerican.com/article/processed-food-a-two-million-year-history/

26. Gerteis J, Izrael D, Deitz D, LeRoy L, Ricciardi R, Miller T, Basu J. *Multiple Chronic Conditions Chartbook. [PDF — 10.62 MB]* AHRQ Publications No, Q14-0038. Rockville, MD: Agency for Healthcare Research and Quality; 2014. Accessed November 18, 2014.

27. Myles, Ian A., *Fast Food Fever: Reviewing the Impacts of the Western Diet on Immunity,* June 17th 2014., https://www.ncbi.nlm.nih.gov/pmc/articles/PMC4074336/

28. Benjamin EJ, Blaha MJ, Chiuve SE, et al. Heart disease and stroke statistics—2017 update: a report from the American Heart Association. *Circulation.* 2017;135:e1–e458

29. National Center for Chronic Disease Prevention and Health Promotion. 06/20/2017 *Chronic Disease Overview* https://www.cdc.gov/chronicdisease/overview/index.htm

30. Rappaport, Stephen M., Genetic Factors Are Not the Major Causes of Chronic Disease. 04/22/2016, https://www.ncbi.nlm.nih.gov/pmc/articles/PMC4841510/

31. Gupta, Sunjay, MD., CBS News, 60 Minutes, Is Sugar Toxic Episode, 04/01/2012 https://www.youtube.com/watch?time_continue=622&v=pxG3YiBMMZE

32. Diabetologia. *A toddler with type 2 diabetes.* ScienceDaily. ScienceDaily, 16 September 2015. www.sciencedaily.com/releases/2015/09/150916215548.htm

33. Marshall, Ron., 09/10/2015, *How Many Ads Do You See in One Day?.* https://www.redcrowmarketing.com/2015/09/10/many-ads-see-one-day/

34. May, Ashley., *Coconut Oil Isn't Healthy. It's Never Been Healthy.,* 06/16/2017. https://www.usatoday.com/story/news/nation-now/2017/06/16/coconut-oil-isnt-healthy-its-never-been-healthy/402719001/

35. Frank M. Sacks, Alice H. Lichtenstein, Jason H.Y. Wu, Lawrence J. Appel, Mark A. Creager, Penny M. Kris-Etherton, Michael Miller, Eric B. Rimm, Lawrence L. Rudel, Jennifer G. Robinson, Neil J. Stone, Linda V. Van Hornand On behalf of the American Heart Association., 06/15/2017., http://circ.ahajournals.org/content/early/2017/06/15/CIR.0000000000000510

36. Adler, Bill., *American Heart Association Enhances Communications / Marketing Organization to Adapt to Changing Media Landscape, Consumers*

Needs., 05/16/2016. http://newsroom.heart.org/news/american-heart-association-enhances-communications-marketing-organization-to-adapt-to-changing-media-landscape-consumer-needs

37.   Aspery, Dave., Why Coconut Oil is Better Than Vegetable Oil., https://blog.bulletproof.com/why-coconut-oil-is-better-than-vegetable-oil/

38.   Kenner, Robert., Pearlstein, Elise., Roberts., Kim., *Food, Inc.*, 2008., http://www.script-o-rama.com/movie_scripts/f/food-inc-script-transcript.html

39.   Hoy., M Katherine., EdD., Goldman., Joseph D., MA., Fiber intake of the U.S. Population., https://www.ars.usda.gov/ARSUserFiles/80400530/pdf/DBrief/12_fiber_intake_0910.pdf

40.   Roger Clemens, Sibylle Kranz, Amy R. Mobley, Theresa A. Nicklas, Mary Pat Raimondi, Judith C. Rodriguez, Joanne L. Slavin, Hope Warshaw; Filling America's Fiber Intake Gap: Summary of a Roundtable to Probe Realistic Solutions with a Focus on Grain-Based Foods, *The Journal of Nutrition*, Volume 142, Issue 7, 1 July 2012, Pages 1390S–1401S, https://doi.org/10.3945/jn.112.160176   https://academic.oup.com/jn/article/142/7/1390S/4630933

41.   Keys., Ancel., *Launching the Seven Countries Study.*, https://www.sevencountriesstudy.com/about-the-study/investigators/ancel-keys/

42.   *de Munter JS, Hu FB, Spiegelman D, Franz M, van Dam RM. Whole grain, bran, and germ intake and risk of type 2 diabetes: a prospective cohort study and systematic review. PLoS Med. 2007;4:e261.*

43.   Leveque, Kelly., *Body Love*, 2017, Harpercollins

44.   Stoppler, Melissa Conrad., MD. Ferry, Robert., Jr. MD., Cunha, John P., *Insulin Resistance.* https://www.medicinenet.com/insulin_resistance/article.htm

45.   Boseley, Sarah., Prozac, Used *by 40m People, Does Not Work Says Scientists*, 02/26/2008., https://www.theguardian.com/society/2008/feb/26/mentalhealth.medicalresearch

46.   Baylor College Of Medicine. *"Study Finds Common Knee Surgery No Better Than Placebo."* ScienceDaily. ScienceDaily, 12 July 2002. www.sciencedaily.com/releases/2002/07/020712075415.htm

47.   Pollan, Michael., *Some of My Best Friends Are Gems.*, 05/15/2013, http://www.nytimes.com/2013/05/19/magazine/say-hello-to-the-100-trillion-bacteria-that-make-up-your-microbiome.html

48.   Hyman, Mark MD., *How to Fix Your Gut Bacteria and Lose Weight.*, http://drhyman.com/blog/2016/02/18/how-to-fix-your-gut-bacteria-and-lose-weight/

49.   The American Gut Project., *Preliminary Characterization of the American Gut Population.*, 11/25/2014., http://americangut.org/wp-content/uploads/2016/02/mod1_main.pdf

50.   Kulecka, Maria et al. *Prolonged Transfer of Feces from the Lean Mice Modulates Gut Microbiota in Obese Mice. Nutrition & Metabolism* 13.1 (2016) : 57. *PMC.* Web. 8 May 2018. https://www.ncbi.nlm.nih.gov/pmc/articles/PMC4995824/

51.   Campbell, Andrew W. *"Autoimmunity and the Gut." Autoimmune Diseases* 2014 (2014) : 152428. *PMC.* Web. 8 May 2018. https://www.ncbi.nlm.nih.gov/pmc/articles/PMC4036413/

52.   Sloan, Mark Dr., *Unintended Consequences: Cesarean Section, The Gut Microbiota, and Child Health.*, 02/15/2017 https://www.scienceandsensibility.org/blog/unintended-consequences-cesarean-section,-the-gut-microbiota,-and-child-health

53.   Stoller-Conrad, Jessica., *Microbes Help Produce Serotonin in Gut.*, 04/09/2015 http://www.caltech.edu/news/microbes-help-produce-serotonin-gut-46495

54.   Oosthoek, Sharon., *Gut Feeling: How Intestinal Bacteria May Influence Our Moods.* 07/14/2014. http://www.cbc.ca/news/gut-feeling-how-intestinal-bacteria-may-influence-our-moods-1.2701037

55.   Sonnenburg, Erica., Sonnenburg, Justin., *"Gut Feelings- The "Second Brain in Our Gastrointestinal Systems."* 05/01/2015.,https://www.scientificamerican.com/article/gut-feelings-the-second-brain-in-our-gastrointestinal-systems-excerpt/

56.   Frontiers. *"Treating autism by targeting the gut."* ScienceDaily. ScienceDaily, 19 June 2017. www.sciencedaily.com/releases/2017/06/170619101834.htm

57.   Li, Qinrui., Han, Ying., Dy, Angel Belle C., Hagerman, Randi J., *"The Gut Microbiota and Autism Spectrum Disorders."* 28 April 2017. https://www.frontiersin.org/articles/10.3389/fncel.2017.00120/full

58.   Qinrui Li, Ying Han, Angel Belle C. Dy, Randi J. Hagerman. *"The Gut Microbiota and Autism Spectrum Disorders".* Frontiers in Cellular Neuroscience, 2017; 11 DOI: 10.3389/fncel.2017.00120

59. American Gut., *Our Results so Far.*, http://americangut.org/our-results-so-far/

60. The Huffington Post UK., *"Being Hyper Hygienic Can Harm Your Immune System And Cause A Surge In Alzheimer's Disease, Experts Say.,"* 05/09/2013., https://www.huffingtonpost.co.uk/2013/09/05/alzheimers-sanitation-immune-system_n_3871358.html

61. Rapin, Jean Robert, and Nicolas Wiernsperger. "Possible Links between Intestinal Permeablity and Food Processing: A Potential Therapeutic Niche for Glutamine." *Clinics* 65.6 (2010) : 635–643. *PMC.* Web. 8 May 2018.https://www.ncbi.nlm.nih.gov/pmc/articles/PMC2898551/

62. Lyte Mark., (2013) Microbial Endocrinology in the Microbiome-Gut-Brain Axis: How Bacterial Production and Utilization of Neurochemicals Influence Behavior. PLoS Pathog 9(11) : e1003726. https://doi.org/10.1371/journal.ppat.1003726 http://journals.plos.org/plospathogens/article?id=10.1371/journal.ppat.1003726

63. Vighi, G et al. "Allergy and the Gastrointestinal System." *Clinical and Experimental Immunology* 153.Suppl 1 (2008) : 3–6. *PMC.* Web. 8 May 2018. https://www.ncbi.nlm.nih.gov/pmc/articles/PMC2515351/

64. WedMD., *"Common Food Allergy Triggers.,"* Table 2 https://www.webmd.com/allergies/food-triggers

65. Axe, Josh Dr., *"Should You Do an Elimination Diet?"* https://draxe.com/elimination-diet/

66. Hartwig, Melissa., *"Whole 30 Program Rules.,"* tps://whole30.com/whole30-program-rules/%5C

67. Hartwig, Melissa., Whole 30., https://whole30.com/

68. Tribole, Evelyn., Resch, Elyse., *Intuitive Eating: A Revolutionary Program that Works.,* 2012. St. Martins Press, Ney York, New York

69. https://www.health.harvard.edu/blog/nutritional-psychiatry-your-brain-on-food-201511168626

70. Stringhini S, Dugravot A, Shipley M, Goldberg M, Zins M, et al. (2011) *Health behaviours, socioeconomic status, and mortality: further analyses of the British Whitehall II and the French GAZEL prospective cohorts. PLoS Med 8: e1000419.*

71. Amino Acids Studies, *"What is Tryptophan"* http://aminoacidstudies.org/L-Tryptophan

72. Simopoulos, Artemis P. "An Increase in the Omega-6/Omega-3 Fatty Acid Ratio Increases the Risk for Obesity." *Nutrients* 8.3 (2016) :

128. *PMC*. Web. 9 May 2018. https://www.ncbi.nlm.nih.gov/pmc/articles/PMC4808858/

73. Osher Y, Belmaker RH., *"Omega-3 Fatty Acids in Depression: A Review of Three Studies"* shttps://www.ncbi.nlm.nih.gov/pubmed/19499625

74. Tarasov EA[1], Blinov DV[1], Zimovina UV[1], Sandakova EA[1]. *"Magnesium deficiency and stress: Issues of Their Relationship Diagnostic Tests, and approaches to Therapy."* https://www.ncbi.nlm.nih.gov/pubmed/26591563

75. Gbyl K[1], Østergaard Madsen H, Dunker Svendsen S, Petersen PM, Hageman I, Volf C, Martiny K. *"Depressed Patients Hospitalized in Southeast-Facing Rooms Are Discharged Earlier than Patients in Northeast-Facing Rooms:* https://www.ncbi.nlm.nih.gov/pubmed/28637044

76. University of Minnesota, *"Minnesota Starvation Experience,"* https://en.wikipedia.org/wiki/Minnesota_Starvation_Experiment

77. The Psychological Science of Self-Control. *"What You Need to Know About Willpower"* http://www.apa.org/helpcenter/willpower.aspx

78. Aamodt, Sandra., *"Why You Can't Lose Weight on a Diet."*

79. Med Broadcast., *"Hypoglycemia."* http://www.medbroadcast.com/condition/getcondition/hypoglycemia

80. Your Hormones, "Cholecystokinin." http://www.yourhormones.info/hormones/cholecystokinin/

81. Magee, Elaine MPH, RD., "Your 'Hunger Hormones.'" https://www.webmd.com/diet/features/your-hunger-hormones#1

82. Aamodt, Sandra., *"Why You Can't Lose Weight on a Diet."* https://www.nytimes.com/2016/05/08/opinion/sunday/why-you-cant-lose-weight-on-a-diet.html

83. Riess, Helen M.D., Dockray-Miller, Mary., Integrative Group Treatment for Bulimia Nervosa. *"Set-Point Theory"* https://medical.mit.edu/sites/default/files/set_point_theory.pdf

84. Benton, David., Young., Hayley A., *"Reducing Calorie Intake May Not Help You Lose Body Weight."* http://journals.sagepub.com/doi/full/10.1177/1745691617690878

85. Hargrove, James L., The Journal of Nutrition., *"History of Calorie in Nutrition."* https://academic.oup.com/jn/article/136/12/2957/4663943

86. United States Department of Agriculture. *"Wilbur Olin Atwater Papers."* https://specialcollections.nal.usda.gov/guide-collections/wilbur-olin-atwater-papers

87. Dietitians Association of Australia. *"The Ins and Outs of Unsaturated Fats."* https://daa.asn.au/smart-eating-for-you/smart-eating-fast-facts/nourishing-nutrients/the-ins-and-outs-of-unsaturated-fats/

88. Blair, Steven N., Department of Exercise Science and Epidemiology/Biostatistics. *"Physical Inactivity: The Biggest Public Health Problem of the 21sy Century."* http://bjsm.bmj.com/content/43/1/1.full

89. Bacon, Linda., *Health at Every Size*. Dallas: BenBella, 2008. Print

90. HCG Diet., *"What is The HCG Diet."* https://hcgdiet.com/what-is-the-hcg-diet/

91. Lowe, Michael R. et al. *"Dieting and Restrained Eating as Prospective Predictors of Weight Gain."* Frontiers in Psychology 4 (2013) : 577. PMC. Web. 9 May 2018. https://www.ncbi.nlm.nih.gov/pmc/articles/PMC3759019/

92. Aamodt, Sandra., *"Why You Can't Lose Weight on a Diet."* May 6, 2016 https://www.nytimes.com/2016/05/08/opinion/sunday/why-you-cant-lose-weight-on-a-diet.html

93. Hyman, Mark MD., *"5 Reasons Most Diets Fail (and How To Succeed."* http://drhyman.com/blog/2014/05/26/5-reasons-diets-fail-succeed/

94. Boston Medical Center., *"Nutrition and Weight Management."* https://www.bmc.org/nutrition-and-weight-management/weight-management

95. Sinek, Simon., *"Consistency or Intensity?"* https://www.youtube.com/watch?v=0NB5y9654qQ

96. Waters, Mark., Wiseman, Rosalind., Fey, Tina., *Mean Girls*

97. Bacon, Linda., *Health at Every Size*. Dallas: BenBella, 2008. Print

98. Bacon, Linda., *Health at Every Size*. Pg. 104., Dallas: BenBella, 2008. Print

99. Pollan, Michael., *"How to Feed the World."* May 19, 2008. https://michaelpollan.com/articles-archive/how-to-feed-the-world/

100. FDA Food and Drug Administration., *"Antimicrobials Sold or Distributed for Use in Food-Producing Animals."* 2009 Summary Report. https://www.fda.gov/downloads/ForIndustry/UserFees/AnimalDrugUserFeeActADUFA/UCM231851.pdf

101. Benbrook, Charles M., Environmental Sciences Europe. *"Trends in Glyphosate Herbicide Use In The United States and Globally."* https://enveurope.springeropen.com/articles/10.1186/s12302-016-0070-0

102. Climate Nexus., *"Animal Agriculture's Impact on Climate Change."* https://climatenexus.org/climate-issues/food/animal-agricultures-impact-on-climate-change/

103. Bost, Jay., *"The Ethicist Contest Winner: Give Thanks for Meat."* May 3, 2012 http://www.nytimes.com/2012/05/06/magazine/the-ethicist-contest-winner-give-thanks-for-meat.html

104. Bacon, Linda., *Health at Every Size*. Dallas: BenBella, 2008. Print

105. The Three Fifths Compromise Summary https://constitution.laws.com/three-fifths-compromise

106. 19th Amendment to the US Constitution., https://www.ourdocuments.gov/doc.php?flash=false&doc=63

107. Elizabeth Cady Stanton https://en.wikipedia.org/wiki/Elizabeth_Cady_Stanton

108. Juran, Joseph M., *"Pareto Principle."* https://en.wikipedia.org/wiki/Pareto_principle

109. Wong, Jowl., Brown, Joshua., *"How Gratitude Changes You and Your Brain."* https://greatergood.berkeley.edu/article/item/how_gratitude_changes_you_and_your_brain

ABOUT THE AUTHOR

C ara Carin Cifelli is a Holistic Health Coach living in Los Angeles, California.

Like many men and women, she used to be very concerned with her weight and body size. She had a very unhealthy relationship with food which made everyday life very challenging and eventually lead to a decade long battle with an eating disorder. Through her challenging, yet in hindsight rewarding, experience she made it her mission to free others from the obsessive, all consuming thoughts about food and their body. In doing so she hopes to transform the cultural conversation that marginalizes those in various body types.

She teaches others how to accept and love the skin they are in, all the while getting deeply connected to what their bodies are telling them aka their Body Wisdom.

You can find some of her work on Recovery Warriors, Elephant Journal, Mind Body Green, and her website www.caraskitchen.net

You can also find her on

Instagram: @caraskitchen

Youtube: Caras Kitchen

Facebook: https://www.facebook.com/carainthekitchen

Made in the USA
Coppell, TX
25 November 2023

24742998R00144